Welcome, Now Leave

Welcome, Now Leave

*How a would-be Shangri-la
went hopelessly cattywampus*

STUART R. WARD

Ward & Quill
Montague, California

ISBN: 978-0-9771754-0-6 (print)
ISBN: 978-0-9771754-2-0 (ebook)

Portions of this book were first published in the
Mt. Shasta Herald on September 22 and 29, 2021.

Ward, Stuart R., 1949 –

The body typeface is set in Adobe Garamond Pro; size 11pt

Published by Ward & Quill
Montague, California

*Dedicated to all who have found
a measure of joy and peace for being in
Mt. Shasta Vista and still wish it well*

Contents

Preface

Entering Mt. Shasta Vista for the first time was like walking into the middle of a movie and trying to figure out the plot — one that seemed by turns written by Zane Grey, Rod Serling and J. Edgar Hoover.

I'm *still* trying to figure out the plot... even after having lived in this peculiar rural development for 47 years. Even after a sea-level change in 2015, when its long-empty lots found sudden, dramatic and controversial new life and purpose, 50 years after its likewise controversial founding, making headlines.

I've come to appreciate how the one-time camping retreat, tucked in the Siskiyou County hinterlands of far Northern California's Mt. Shasta region, has its own distinct personality — a unique energy matrix — regardless of who is currently residing or visiting. And its own unique *doom loop*, which is defined as "a self-reinforcing cycle where one negative factor triggers another, worsening the situation, creating a downward spiral."

The following deep-dive pieces together the place's origins and tries to determine how and why it went so profoundly astray, ages before the relatively recent quantum shift to serving as a rogue commercial pot-growing haven ever happened. Along the way, I share anecdotes, insights and history gleaned from my many decades living here. The informal, time-jumping story of the Vista (as many residents called it, and as I often refer to it here) was driven in part by a determination to make sense of a place I've called home for over 80% of my adult life, and in part for the chance to indulge my penchants for creative writing, time travel and select analysis.

While touching on events unfolding during and since the 2015 meltdown (which happened to coincide with its 50th anniversary; coincidence?), more controversial events, like the 2021 water-truck ban and the fatal shooting by authorities during the 2022 Lava Fire, all widely covered by media, are omitted; they were yet too raw and unprocessed in mind to be integrated into the narrative.

My main goal: try to determine the root causes that, directly or indirectly, set off the chain reaction of its many subsequent misadventures. While primary focus is on the first 50 years — its antediluvian period, as it were, before the flood of emboldened growers submerged the realm's former age — it also explores how the anticipated legalization of recreational cannabis in California led to that flood. And, as it relates, it examines such subjects as the Uniform Building Code, the regional real estate market, systemic racism, radical body freedom, the power grid and early solar-electric.

The time before I arrived in 1978 — some seven years after the first modern-day settlers began their ephemeral, seemingly idyllic retirement community following the first years of camping-only — has always mystified me. It represented the great unknown, a grand riddle needing to be solved. What happened during that time to create such a peculiar directional arc that affects the place to this day?

Consider this writing 85% casual history and 15% memoir

by one with an abiding love-hate relationship with the place. Having grown like Topsy from an article series I wrote for the local paper in 2021, it's not presented in the neatest linear time-line. Instead, it often timeskips around the decades as nearly half a century of remembered events and new insights came to mind and were added. Secure your seat belt, and this should pose no problem. See it as a topsy-turvy carnival ride time-traveling through the singular history of the remote hideaway that has alternately baffled, intrigued, enamored and repelled visitors and residents alike for 60 years.

I gained insight into the early years by hearing stories from longtime residents, such as my late, mile-distant, neighbor Bill Waterson, who died at 98 in 2016, and by sifting through a complete set of archived *Vistascope* biannual newsletters.

What *did* happen during those critical first years? What led the peculiar place's first vacationers and, later, its residents, to dive down the rabbit hole with such abandon that it became the wildly dysfunctional, anarchistic place it is today? Drawing on firsthand knowledge, findings from various sources, and at least semi-informed deductions, I think I might've found some answers.

Did I use AI? Some. The cover was a joint creation by me, the good folks at Wordzworth and ChatGPT. And while I used Grammarly to help fine-tune *existing* writing, I discovered it had its limitations after it suggested ways to improve a quote from Shakespeare.

Stuart R. Ward

MT. SHASTA VISTA
DECEMBER 31, 2025

…the past is never truly past…it is always tugging up both its treasures and its tragedies and carrying them insistently into the future.

–MARGARET RENKL,
AMERICAN WRITER

[The Vista is]… our home away from home, our frontier, our Shangri-la…there should be a constant flurry of barbecue parties, coffee klatches and just informal get-togethers all through the year.

–GEORGE COLLINS,
FOUNDING DEVELOPER AND FELLOW CAMPER

*Do I contradict myself? Very well then I contradict myself,
(I am large, I contain multitudes.)*

–WALT WHITMAN,
"SONG OF MYSELF," LEAVES OF GRASS

CHAPTER 1

Wilderness condo, anyone?

The archway spanning the main entrance beckoned. Bearing the words "Mt. Shasta Vista" in six-inch scrolled wooden lettering, it made your more whimsical first-timers driving under it imagine they were perhaps entering an enchanted realm or quaint scout retreat — rather than, in fact, a simple, sprawling subdivision of individually-owned, mostly undeveloped recreational lots, with a few homes hidden away among them.

One felt the hopes and dreams that went into that archway. How the place's earliest property owners — first only visiting summers from distant cities for extended camping and rendezvous — had developed a deep affection for their fledgling primitive development, so neatly tucked in the high-desert wooded foothills of Mount Shasta's northwestern slopes.

Begun in the mid-1960s, it was 15 miles out from both Weed and Grenada, off County Road A-12. Its wider region, before long ago being cleared for farming, ranching and charcoal production for smithy forges, was blanketed with Western juniper trees. It was, appropriately enough, named Juniper Flats.

Happy campers turn modern-day settlers

So smitten by its charms were some among the flock of mostly older repeat vacationers, mainly from the Los Angeles area, that they actually decided to retire here. Collectively, they'd segue their individual lots from simple first-generation recreational use into a proto-community of full-on, code-legal residences.

This wasn't as outlandish a move as it might've appeared. At the time of formation, the county had already rezoned the land to single-family residential use in response to the land developer's petition. The community-building venture by the few dozen lot holders was possibly launched in hopes by at least some that like-minded others would follow suit and become self-reliant like them, covering their own water, electrical and sewage-disposal needs, and thus help grow the embryonic rustic settlement. Perhaps over time they could develop a more systematic and centralized infrastructure. Perhaps not.

Meanwhile, it would be up to each prospective resident to provide their own water, power and waste-disposal to meet the then-rigorously enforced building codes. They appeared to envision creating a standard, albeit sparsely settled, backwoods community of respectable, financially secure nature lovers willing to work together in common cause.

This at least *appeared* to be the starry-eyed dream. If so, alas, things didn't exactly pan out. Though a few dozen retiring couples successfully built homes, initial efforts failed to create any common infrastructure beyond a few isolated power and telephone lines and an informal community well. This wouldn't bode well for further standard settlement among the embarrassment of empty lots.

Among the many reasons why things stalled:

- bitterness by locals surrounding the land sale to the developer, in effect putting a whammy on the place from the start;

- the speculating developer, overambitious, creating a super-sized subdivision that held far more lots than the private market could absorb for practical use, even for simple camping;

- lot owners' fallout over a campaign to bring electricity to every lot breaking down the initial, tenuously unified efforts of a majority of lot owners hoping to increase lot values, aggravated by almost certain skyrocketing cost to extend power lines past the initial homebuilding effort;

- the high cost of drilling often-deep wells to hit often-scarce potable water; and

- the arrival of younger, rebellious countercultural back-to-the-landers merrily bent on ignoring health and building codes like they didn't exist

Long story short, forces would conspire to torpedo the fondest dreams of the modern-day settlers. Their vision, seemingly rich in promise, was never fully realized. Instead, the place morphed into a haphazard, semi-zombie development. Theirs proved to be only a short-lived idyllic enclave of transplanted retired city folks before things went seriously awry. No more than maybe six percent of the parcels ever got connected to the grid. And the cost of drilling individual wells often proved so high, and finding affordable water so iffy, that bold noncompliance with health and building codes became increasingly common over time.

The brief idyllic honeymoon of the fledgling respectable community would thus be cut short as it mutated into a bizarre limbo land, becoming an incongruous oil-and-water mix of fully code-compliant residences and decidedly code-challenged ones set adrift amid a sea of empty lots.

Result: The Vista was perpetually in hot water with the county over code violations. And forever at war with itself.

The possibilities!

It seems that the developer, George Collins, was perhaps a gambler at heart and, again, a tad over-ambitious. He'd decided to play it by ear, lacking any disclosed long-range plans or vision for the place and its 1,641 (count 'em) lots, which averaged a generous two and a half acres each. That is, beyond their serving as a simple — read primitive — collectively owned and maintained, de facto recreational resort. While the place always had the *option* to grow into something more, it would be on the lot owners' own dime to provide the required water, electricity hook-up and approved waste systems.

The situation was perfectly legal under California's then-existing, incredibly lax regulations.

Then, on the wings of the Vista's launch, Lake Shastina, a full-on residential development with infrastructure and amenities out the yin-yang, sprang up practically next door. Indeed, new rural subdivisions would soon be springing up across the region as interest in rural living took off. The idea of building residences in such a place was becoming more attractive as more and more people burned out on urban living.

The developer joined the campers

The L.A. developer actually joined the select group of owners in early camping visits. Together, they reveled in extended annual sojourns from afar, gathering to mingle, form work parties and brainstorm the place's possibilities while falling under the mountain's spell. So much so, they must've said, "Hey, we're getting ready to retire; why don't we just pull up stakes and build our own retirement community here? We'll have the wherewithal once we sell our homes. Why not? What could go wrong?"

But surely the group knew it would take a critical mass of lot owners — some of whom bought the parcels to serve as affordable, simple camping retreats, many more as only long-term investments or short-term speculations — if hoping to ever generate enough momentum to bring in more than a few scattered, mostly isolated residences amid an over-abundance of unimproved lots. If unsuccessful, the remaining parcels, no longer ideal for camping and too costly or isolated to build to code on for most, would become more than a skosh problematic.

Indeed, their moving on the land failed to spark any widespread enthusiasm to build likewise: Over 1,500 lots, the overwhelming majority of whose owners soon no longer had any use for them, either for camping or building on, became soured investments and suffered the sorry fate of becoming white elephants.

Almost overnight, the sprawling development effectively turned into one ginormous, all but useless (albeit still charming) real estate desert.

Probably, even in the grand excitement of brainstorming and resolving to leave the smoggy L.A. region behind, they knew they were taking a chance. They'd be unable to hammer out any formal development plans since they represented less than two percent of the owner membership. Willy-nilly was their only option as they winged it, scrambling to build and establish new homes in the strange new land. But they must've been confident — optimistic winds at their backs and plenty of money — that good intentions, bolstered by upright constitutions and rigorous adherence to following codified building requirements, would carry the day in successfully forging a brand-spanking-new rural hamlet for themselves.

Grand reality check

People, myself included, had always assumed the first settlers envisioned growing a thriving rural community over time. Surely they wouldn't want 98% of the lots to sit idle, would they? But the more I thought about it, the more I wondered if among these first settlers were at least some, perhaps even most, who had no vision at all of growing a residency per se.

Possibly, instead, they'd hoped, once each had carved out their own rustic estate, only to further cultivate their existing simpatico circle, never giving thought to building community beyond what their tight-knit group of friends, associates, and family members constituted. Scrambling modern-day pioneers in a challenging new land, it was enough to look to their own interests. So they'd stake their territory in no uncertain terms and let the devil take the hindmost as far as the fate of the rest of the lots and their owners' use of them was concerned for anything beyond brief camp use… or 100% code compliance if opting to join their transplanted SoCal culture.

The firstcomers, newly retired, were psyched at the prospect of withdrawing from the rat-race chaos of a fast-paced world and enjoying their golden years in the peaceful quietude the former campgrounds had earlier provided and what they maybe hoped would now become their own little congenial country club of sorts. The fewer public improvements — "who needs a community center? We can rotate get-togethers in each other's homes" — the better. It'd make it less likely that non simpatico strangers would ever want to move in their cliquish midst with its retiring ways and urbane La-La-Land mindset. And need to be reckoned with for having intruded on the place's tranquil backwoods air and possibly threatening their newfound and much-coveted serenity.

Maybe some banked on there being few others who would be so extravagantly minded, willing to go full-bore like them and build similar legal residences with their steep well-drilling costs and other infrastructure outlays. So they'd be left to enjoy their new secluded lifestyle amid some 1,500 now-defunct recreational properties.

Maybe all along they'd been intent on creating their own exclusive, gated rural community — *only one without gates*. In their place, barking signs would be posted everywhere, hopefully proving sufficient to protect the fledgling retiree scene from unwelcome visitors… and, more importantly, any would-be, intrusive, non-compliant newcomers. Their signs reflected suspicion toward any unknown property owners who might be tempted to ignore the building code for being such secluded parcels in the middle of nowhere. The signs seemed to all but shout:

**Welcome, if you've the bucks to
build a legal residence like us…
otherwise, keep the hell out**

CHAPTER 2

No nothing

At the start it must have appeared little more than a Good Sam's Club of sorts, tucked away in the sleepy hinterlands. An unassuming rural development offering weary smog-choked city dwellers a mess of secluded, affordable, two- to three-acre wooded parcels. A place where now and then one could enjoy relaxed camping, unwind from city cares, mingle with other campers (many or most of whom one already knew, having bought their lots as a group), and breathe fresh high-desert air while soaking in the mountain's quiet majesty.

There was no water, no electricity, no sewer system, no gas, no phone lines. Forget any paved roads or a community center, public park or playground. There was nothing but a lot of lots. Plus a labyrinthine 66-mile network of modest red cinder roads, primitive signage (and one dauntingly tiny map) to access them all.

Called ranch roads by the developer, they were fragile affairs built up of loose rock base over often-deep, sandy soil, with a red cinder topping supplied from a nearby cinder supply operation. As they were never designed to withstand constant heavy loads or frequent or fast traffic, a non-enforceable 15 mph speed limit (being private roads) was posted to help preserve them. Plus, keep the backwoods atmosphere relaxed and tranquil and reduce the dust. Ongoing maintenance was covered by then-modest annual mandatory-membership lot assessments, informally called road dues, levied on the lots' title holders.

It was a sea of turn-key primitive wilderness camping condos, if you will, with what at first appeared to hold no more than a wispy dream of maybe someday growing into something more, maybe not. But a few lot owners — those who actually made use of their new properties, or who were waiting until others developed the place some before jumping in — no doubt imagined the possibilities all along. They were inspired by the secluded lots with their sweeping mountain views. If they moved fast and built homes on their parcels, maybe they could essentially have the whole place all to themselves (along with, again, anyone else willing to do the same).

Converging forces

To better understand the peculiar history of the Vista, it helps to appreciate the forces in play at its formation:

- First and foremost, the late Sixties through the early Seventies were an extraordinarily tumultuous period of social and political upheaval, and a grand, if fitful, mass awakening of human consciousness; a giddy exhilaration and boundless euphoria often filled the air.

- The land possessed a pronounced dreamy quality, aided and abetted by mystical Mt. Shasta, which could easily lead one to imagine the sky was the limit for its development, with little need to attend to any mundane details.

- The historic Back-to-the-Land movement was accelerating as many were fleeing urban areas to live closer to nature, seeking rustic tranquility and a simpler way of life.

- Again, beyond simple road access, state regulations of the day didn't require new rural subdivisions to supply diddly-squat.

Combine these — along with the Vista's super-affordable lot prices encouraging impulsive purchases lacking any focused intent beyond hoping values might rise or maybe using for camping — and you perhaps had a more than passing possibility that some improbable, strange-magic lotus land like the Vista would emerge. A place where the baby-boomer inhabitants who soon followed the first wave of convention-minded dwellers could merrily pursue bohemian living deep in the bosom of nature, tuning out any uptight persnickety neighbors or tedious downers like building codes lurking beyond its borders.

Country comfort

Situated a few miles uphill and northeast of the soon-to-be exurb of Lake Shastina, many of the realm's parcels held a profoundly still, dreamlike air of solitude (or mind-numbingly stark isolation, depending on one's mindset). As most lots were one to five miles in from its five blacktop entrances with their tranquility-eroding traffic wash, one might've felt as if they were 100 miles, rather than the actual 15, from the nearest town.

The embarrassment of wooded high-desert lots was spread over nearly seven square miles of mostly juniper and sagebrush, with the occasional cluster or solo stand of tall Ponderosa and Jeffrey pine. Terrain was sometimes rocky and hilly, relatively rock-free and flat to gently sloping, sometimes a blend of the two. It spanned nearly six miles between its furthest points, and National Forest or Bureau of Land Management lands flanked many of its borders, further lending a wilderness feel to the place. The square-mile sections were in two giant clumps, separated by a square mile of federal BLM land and County Highway A-12, which ran diagonally between the second, smaller grouping of Sections 23 and 13, near Pluto Caves and Sheep Rock, respectively.

As was often the case with such rural subdivisions, the development team had conjured whimsical road names, hoping to tickle the fancy of their target market: private vacation land seekers, impulsive, casual land investors and those seeking potential rural home or cabin sites. Evocative names like White Cloud Road, Zane Gray Drive and Happy Lane. Rich-sounding names like Silver Lode Road, Golden Road, Lost Mine Road and Bonanza Drive. One, Rosebud Lane, was perhaps a nod to the cryptic utterance in the movie, *Citizen Kane*. Another was a shameless pun of the 1960s' "Rawhide" TV series theme song belter: Frankie Lane.

A few were named after saints, like St. George Drive and St. Mary Road, perhaps lending the development the air of being an unlikely Catholic summer camp. Collins Drive and McLarty Road were named after the developer and his leading man. A third, Ragan Drive, was named after the local realtor who joined forces with them to move the sea of parcels. For all anyone knew, some roads, like Mildred Drive or Dottie Lane, were named after one's wife, sweetheart or perhaps the namer's mad crush from third grade.

Born amid controversy:
Place was an instant problem child

The development officially came into existence on November 3, 1965, going by the date on which formal paperwork was filed and time-stamped at the Siskiyou County courthouse. (I used this date rather than the earlier, yet-to-be-filed incorporation date of August 18, 1965.) The brainchild of developer George Collins's Southern California-based outfit, Pacific Shores Realty, it was on land he purchased from one of the many descendants of the California Gold Rush pioneer R.M. Martin (likely a great-great-grandson or some such) who had made it big in cattle, and whose family members long held much of the broader region he'd acquired. They grazed their livestock on the wild lands, seasonally making short cattle drives right down the middle of the future development's then-uber-sleepy flanking two-lane highway. Old cow patties still littered the parcels over a decade after the Vista's start.

The unfenced area had been considered among the best hunting grounds in the entire 6,278-square-mile county (California's fifth-largest) for over a century. And before white settlers came, American Indians seasonally hunted through the mostly waterless area; I found a complete obsidian arrowhead on my parcel the very first week. More recently, the region was picked clean of most of its tall pines by lumber baron Abner Weed around the turn of the last century; there were a few large stumps on my lot still leisurely decomposing, some 80 years later.

Family and locals were reportedly outraged by the sale

With each new generation, the pioneer's vast land holdings were further divided among family members, doubtless hoping to keep the land in the family. Still, each owner must have had the right, however distasteful it might've been, to sell their holding if they wanted. The story went that when Jess Martin sold his seven square miles of prime wooded land to Collins, other family members were furious. But they were powerless to stop the sale and the commercial nonsense set in motion on their now-lost ancestral holding. The region's other long-time residents, intimately familiar with the unfenced land, in turn expressed similar rage at the disruption to their bucolic lifestyle. The sale represented a jarring disturbance to every long-established resident's nostalgic rural identity.

This eruption of ill feeling over the land sale flared up *long* before the handful of lot owners ever tried to morph the de facto primitive resort into a quasi-exclusive rural retirement village. Long before they'd find themselves engaged in a take-no-prisoners war with the code-ignoring land buyers who'd dare to move in on the cheap, invading what the former would by then consider to be *their* domain.

This reported controversy surrounding the very land sale would set the stage for all subsequent troubles. It laid a faulty foundation for the world of persistent contention and confusion destined to practically define the place in the public eye.

In other words, the place never had a chance.

Greenlit by the county supervisors...
to their eternal regret

Long-ensconced locals grumbled how their longtime backwoods hunting, camping and grazing backwoods were being permanently closed off just so a bunch of rich big-city folk could lollygag about in shiny Airstreams a few weeks a year, Meanwhile, wheels were turning at the county courthouse.

The county's then four-member board of supervisors must've sympathized with the aggrieved Martin family members and fuming locals. Perhaps they had initially been skeptical of approving it. But due to Collins's persistence, earnest assurances, proven track record of successfully launching subdivisions elsewhere, and the county board's frugality, given that Siskiyou was California's third-poorest county per capita, they must've either been won over or were unable to think of a valid reason *not* to approve it. The land had already been rezoned, anyhow; the project was already in the pipeline. They were no doubt keenly aware of the fresh revenue stream that 1,641 individually owned and taxed lots would bring to the county's coffers (at the cost of additional recordkeeping and paperwork), especially if improvements were made on them.

Concerns had been raised about the possible lack of dependable water and the parcels' often rocky, volcanic nature, which might make owners hard-pressed to accommodate conventional septic systems should they ever want to build. The board insisted his team first drill test wells to demonstrate the land had sufficient water. They must've finally decided that it at least *appeared* to have enough and trusted that any future home builders, exercising due diligence, would realize that the cost of bringing in wells and electricity might be prohibitive. They trusted common sense and dutiful compliance with county ordinances would prevail.

So while the board approved the development in a three-to-one vote once other requested specifications, such as enlarging the turnaround diameter of the cul-de-sacs, had been addressed, the one dissenting supervisor, Mr. Jackson, appeared to remain skeptical. One of the test wells Collins drilled was at the highest elevation in Section 13, below Sheep Rock, to show that there was likely water everywhere *if* one went deep enough; it had drawn only five gallons a minute — the minimum to be deemed a practical well. Jackson may have thought that wasn't enough to assure the place could provide adequate water if vacationers wanted to sink wells and so avoid hauling in the precious, heavy liquid. Or, more importantly, for possible would-be home builders, for whom having a dependable water supply was the most crucial requirement to become eligible for a building permit.

It's the water

His skepticism proved justified in time. He might've had to refrain from saying "I told you so" to fellow board members.

(That is, assuming his lone dissenting vote wasn't only a calculated sop to appease the infuriated citizenry.) While many future residents hit water between 200 and 300 feet in the lower sections, and often in one higher one, Section 13, the required drilling depths in the other, Section 23, could reach *700 feet or more*. And even then, some wells, regardless of depth, might be plagued by iron content that turned white laundry sheets pink, or worse, arsenic, requiring expensive filtering systems to render the water safe for drinking.

A retired couple on Gilman Road, Buzz and Helen Kehner, lived a mile away from me. They'd drilled a super-deep well, some 700 feet down. Its water had arsenic levels within the then-acceptable health department limit *if* first treated with rock salt filtration, which they did. Not many years later, they both died, and not that far apart. While I never learned if arsenic poisoning was determined to be a contributing factor or leading cause in their deaths, the county health department drastically reduced future wells' acceptable arsenic levels not long after.

Shifting attitudes

The county authorities' faith in lot buyers to be law-abiding and do the right thing was about to be sorely tried. Over time, their attitudes towards the soon-beleaguered realm would shift markedly. Initial thoughtful, cautious concern first gave way to frustration. Then it grew to exasperation. As matters escalated, newcomers openly ignoring health and building codes, sentiment turned to open hostility. Finally, as the county realized it had a perpetual problem child on its hands, it settled back into a rueful, *oh-hell-what-can-any-one-do-about-the-misbegotten-place* dismissiveness and callous disregard.

They were mad at the place and its bickering owners. They were mad at their predecessors for being foolish enough to ever approve it. And they were mad at themselves for lacking the wherewithal to effectively enforce their own statutes should enough people choose to ignore them.

Although it was later events that would *really* aggravate authorities, the downward spiral in sentiment — beyond grumbling locals likely influencing their views — was undoubtedly first triggered by the conspicuous lack of water. It would, directly or indirectly, lead to almost all future problems. The subsequent willful disregard of residential living standards only drove the local government's already present exasperation and displeasure over the misbegotten place through the roof. Ill regard and indifference towards its eventual, seemingly hopeless dysfunctionality, replete with chronically infighting residents forever demanding that officials intervene, spread to every last county department, with of course the exception of the tax collector's office.

An electrifying turn of events

Between the original landowners' and locals' bitter resentment over their lost stomping grounds and the scarce water, scarce power and often rocky ground, all of which made code compliance extra challenging and costly for any new owners thinking to build, an already fraught situation was on its way to snowballing even further out of control.

The handful of ambitious and adventurous lot owners who'd brainstormed the idea of settling on their parcels, retiring as an urbane, ostensibly congenial group of one-time shared-vacation buddies, were a scrupulously law-abiding lot. Each dutifully first drilled an approved well, paid into a volunteer-assessment power-and-light fund to help cover the cost of extending power lines, and installed an approved septic system.

Each thereby provided all necessary infrastructure individually before applying for a home-building permit. This was issued only after submitting a detailed construction plan for approval, paying a non-refundable fee and agreeing to build in a timely manner. Their generation, having weathered World War II with its monumental civilian cooperation required to support the high-stakes effort to preserve democracy worldwide, was accustomed to dutifully toeing the line without question whenever it came to established authority.

Though a few might've been hands-on owner-builders who stayed on-site during construction, most had likely hired contractors and lived elsewhere until their houses were completed and officially signed off by the county building department.

On its way

At first glance, it might have appeared that the place was well on its way to becoming a respectable, if ultra-sparsely settled, community. Telephone lines were extended to the developing lots, along with a few scattered power lines, sometimes the two sharing the same poles. Those with green thumbs planted colorful flowers at the highway entrances. It seemed everyone knew everyone; theirs was a close-knit community, emerging into a happy hideaway for the flock of excited, newly retired dwellers from afar who together had made the bold leap.

But the change, again, came at the price of spoiling the widespread first-generation lot use as secluded retreats, for which purpose no doubt many had bought lots. Such owners had no interest in even building *fences*, let alone living structures. The place was just too isolated, too water-challenged, too non-electrified and tall-tree bereft to seriously consider. They must've hoped things would stay primitive so they could continue enjoying the lots for simple camping forays, maybe turn friends on to them, and, ideally, readily sell the lots to other camping enthusiasts if they wanted. They wanted things to remain affordable: no special assessments to try "improving" things.

You didn't mess with success

In their book the place already had all it needed: simple road access. Though the lots *were* technically zoned for single-family residential use, they seemed so perfect for secluded getaways and retreats that it was hard to imagine them being used for anything else, You didn't mess with success, trying to turn a place into something it wasn't well suited for. Especially when far too few lot owners appeared willing to commit to the level of effort and expense required to make a successful transition from collective, primitive campground into a standard community. One with all the bells and whistles city dwellers took for granted and were so unabashedly hooked on: water, electricity and waste-disposal systems.

Not if they were required to supply them all themselves, at their own expense, for the foreseeable future.

Maybe the majority by then realized that the place, having lost its idyllic campground charm, would likely never be anything more than a cozy confederation of a few dozen property holders who'd had the bucks and motivation to move fast and become legal residents. Residents who suddenly, irrevocably changed the place's very nature.

The new dwellers, in turn, must have realized that some, if not most, of the 98% of lot owners who didn't join them would be more than a tad upset over how the place had been effectively co-opted. How their tiny group had radically repurposed it and essentially left others in the lurch. They surely knew the primitive situation would discourage others from following suit and building on the challenging lots, and that, therefore, lot values would plummet as their sellability came to a screeching halt.

Yes, it was unfortunate. But that's the way the cookie crumbles. It was everyone for themselves; you snooze, you lose; such is life; c'est la vie; it is what it is…

CHAPTER 3

Not another Lake Shastina

Many absentee lot owners, sensing the place's future prospects appeared sketchy, no doubt didn't want to sink another penny in the place. And so they'd passed on the request for volunteer donations to build up a power-and-light fund. Others maybe didn't want to support what they might've viewed as a capricious, ill-advised changing of horses in the middle of the creek.

With the prospect of losing the pristine charms of their ephemeral sweet-spot hideaways staring them in the face, they'd refused to chip into the voluntary assessment power-and-light fund Collins rallied for. Camping out in open view of someone's large living room window wouldn't have been a particularly enticing prospect. Though the brief, ambitious campaign to bring power to every parcel thus failed for this and other reasons, the 1,000-plus individual contributions had at least enabled stringing power lines to the lots of the few dozen Johnny-on-the-spot retiring couples going for the gusto.

Chomping at the bit

Flush with cash from selling their big-city homes and chomping at the bit to move onto the secluded land they'd fallen in love with, they'd been primed to move fast and simplify their lives; they were ready to fully forsake city living and create their own little rural retirement hamlet. They doubtless envisioned luxuriating happily ever after amid the splendor of year-round woodland solitude in their transplanted So-Cal congeniality — while, staunch, upright citizens they were, holding highest regard for strict law and order. It would become a place that, to all appearances, was open to all comers willing to meet the legal residential building standards, as they had, and join their swell little group.

But nobody else had better even think about it.

Due to the high cost of extending power to lots, most of which were miles away from existing lines, the firstcomers quickly exhausted the fund that so many contributed to, hoping it would still be there when they were ready to build, or for the parties they hoped to sell their lots to at a higher profit. It's unclear whether it was intended as only the first round of contributions, as far greater cash infusions obviously would've been needed to electrify the entire place.

The volunteer fund had likely been established only after Collins realized he couldn't get the two-thirds of lot-owner votes needed to pass a mandatory assessment; I doubt he even tried running it up the flagpole. Maybe the power company had tenuously agreed to offer a discounted, or at least a locked-in, extension rate if everyone got on board and committed to wiring the whole place through such an ongoing special assessment. It would have been a no-brainer indication that there were a significant number of new energy-thirsty customers itching to settle, or at least seriously invest in improvements, as was then happening in just-down-the-hill Lake Shastina, (Random fact: Lake Shastina, once known by the slightly less euphonious name of Dwinnell Reservoir, was created by damming up Shasta River and diverting flows of Parks Creek and Carrick Creek in 1927, along with building a long cross-country canal outlet to aid regional alfalfa and hay farmers and create pasture land.)

Hoping to goose parcel values

Beyond the handful of early house builders and mobile home installers, those considering building in the future, and lot holders who'd hoped to keep the place dedicated to primitive retreat use, were others, almost certainly the overwhelming majority. This group had seemed keen on segueing the giant checkerboard of infrastructure-bereft parcels into an actual, by-golly residential community. Or at least further develop their potential to become one by first expanding it into a seasonal rural backwoods resort with additional amenities like electricity and water, perhaps a small grocery and gas station. But not for their own use. *Are you kidding? Perish the thought.* No, they were merely disinterested speculators hoping to goose market values.

Regardless of what some owners thought about the abrupt shift in land use and the embryonic rural community soon more or less claiming the territory as their own, that tiny handful of owners of a certain age — with the means and resolve to move fast and create their own bare-bones, de facto rural retirement village, new homes sometimes companionably clustered, other times a quarter mile or more apart — had gone for it lock, stock and barrel.

Soon after, though, the power company withdrew its tentative commitment. They'd realized there was no groundswell of landholders keen on settling the land, only the thinnest scattering. The place showed early signs of becoming a serious developmental misfire. But owners hoping to build in the future might've thought they could live with the power company's withdrawal; they'd just pay for an affordable line extension later.

Power extension costs were likely about to skyrocket

A growing spirit of contention over bringing in power had divided lot owners early on, along with a loss of confidence in the developer who'd pushed for everyone to chip into the fund, hoping to get everyone on board and thus possibly securing a solid commitment to wire the entire place. He might've thought that — in a dime, in a dollar — they'd agree to further, maybe soon mandatory, assessments down the road to keep the fund solvent. Thus, over time, power would've indeed been brought to every lot in the over-ambitious back-of-beyond hideaway.

But if he had learned that line-extension costs were about to skyrocket, he would've realized there was a limited window, once-in-a-lifetime chance to wire the whole place at an affordable price.

Staggering increase?

A friend of mine, Omar Dickenson, had lived in the backwoods of upstate New York about the same time. He told me that, immediately after he had his family's lines extended, his power supplier increased the extension price from 50 cents to $5 a foot — *a staggering tenfold increase*. As it turned out, this was a national trend and likely the case here as well. This would've created an especially discouraging double whammy for any would-be Vistan settler. First, the fund was drained. Then the region's power company, Pacific Power, was probably demanding prohibitively high extension fees, leaving any would-be home, cabin, or mobile home builder or installer reeling after having relied on continued affordable rates.

But it wasn't as if the power company, assuming the steep increase did occur, was getting greedy all of a sudden. In earlier times, the costs of extending power were predictable and often subsidized by government programs. And companies were primarily involved in connecting denser populations to their high-voltage go-juice. Relatively inexpensive, clean hydropower had long supplied the Northwest through the massive Columbia Basin Project. By the 1970s, though, amid high inflation, rising equipment costs and growing populations, power companies had to seek new, more costly energy sources — primarily coal and gas — to boost output and diversify operations to meet growing demand. Also, they were less able to absorb investment costs. Result: To remain solvent, they were compelled to charge *considerably* higher fees for further power line extensions, and maybe they factored in a higher rate for supplying new lines to widely scattered rural dwellers.

Molten rage

In any event, it turned out that over 1,000 Vistan property owners had effectively subsidized the electrical hookup costs of a few dozen. It no doubt struck some as unfair (though having been advised it was first-come, first-served, good 'til gone). Tempers were already frayed over being asked for more money over the prospect of ruining a nice co-op campground with unsightly power poles and wires, driving up costs while destroying the usability of what were once charming hideaways.

Now, if Pacific Power were now indeed demanding an arm and a leg for further line extensions, lot holders would've erupted in molten rage to match the intensity of the long-ago lava spewing forth from the place's namesake dormant volcano. (More random facts: According to scientific carbon dating, Mt. Shasta's most recent eruption occurred about 1250 AD; the last major event, though, was some 3,200 years ago. It's erupted at least once every 800 years over the past 10,000 years; do the math.)

Some might have erroneously concluded that the developer had intentionally misrepresented the financial realities involved in electrifying the place, only to aid the homesteading ambitions of a few he'd gotten cozy with. Or had otherwise fudged the facts, promising something he knew he couldn't deliver. Or, most cynically, they perhaps decided he had no idea *what* he was doing. In contrast, some no doubt felt he was blameless, having done his level best to advance the interests of the property owners as a whole. And the power company, too; it had no choice but to raise extension prices if it hoped to continue serving the electrical needs of a growing population amid rampant inflation, dwindling cheap hydro and declining government subsidies.

Whatever the reasons, lot holders were increasingly upset over the sorry state of affairs. The sweet divergent dreams of Vista camping *and* homebuilding were both turning sour fast.

Lookin' for a home in the country...
when worlds collide

Into this growing hornets' nest of resentments, jealousies, misgivings, disillusionment and sundry disconnects already plaguing the development, handicapping its lots' potential market values, then entered a whole new breed of lot owner. One destined to put the proverbial cherry on top: instant homesteaders. Young back-to-the-landers, long on rebellious attitudes and often short on cash.

The mid- to late 1960s' through the early 1970s' historical Back-to-the-Land movement was initially sparked by a rapidly emerging counterculture whose members were burned out on an increasingly industrialized and desensitized urban lifestyle and wanted to get back to nature... *seriously* back to nature. A rising tide of the population was primed to flee Babylon (as some put it biblically). Its number soon cut across class lines. Indeed, the first excited residents, themselves having had their own fill of urban living, had gotten swept up in it. If untouched nature is so nice to visit so often, why not just live in it full-time and be done?

But, alas, in Vista's case, it was a luxurious notion only the comfortably situated could afford to pursue *if* one intended to conform to the costly, then strictly enforced, county health and building codes. Codes that were made all the more expensive due to the lack of easy water, the daunting lack of electrical lines, and terrain often making approved septic systems problematic.

As anyone who lived through those purple-haze daze remembers (if not overdoing pot and psychedelics), even while it was a time of astonishingly polarized and wrenching social and cultural upheaval and deadly wars, there was at the same time an amazingly powerful magic afoot, a rapidly emerging awareness of life's infinite possibilities.

A once-in-26,000-years event?

Esoteric teachings held that a momentous new 26,000-year cycle — the physical procession of the equinoxes, believed to affect human consciousness and evolution — was beginning. It was a time of ecstatic celebration over the considered start of a new Great Year, even if most people didn't realize at the time the cause of the times' wildly inspired merriment and phenomenal renewed passion for living.

A stream of young, often financially struggling, freedom-minded, in-your-face, nonconformist dreamers was inspired to make the great escape from teeming cities. They sought simple country living to heal and free their spirits. It was only a matter of time before they, too, would discover the same generously sized, secluded lots with their namesake's sweeping views and irresistibly affordable prices that had earlier lured the Vista's first modern-day settlers.

Some, and eventually most, of the younger newcomers apparently would prove intent on ignoring the deemed unreasonable codes, regulations and restrictions that dedicated bureaucrats and lawmakers had so painstakingly crafted and codified. They were scorned as needlessly expensive and ridiculously oppressive. Such codes would require a person to first drill what might prove to be a 700-foot well, pay an exorbitant price to have power lines extended, and build a living structure to meet steep code requirements, all before ostensibly having the right to remain on their own property for more than 30 days a year. Or create anything more than a fence without first obtaining and paying for a building permit and submitting detailed plans for some detached city bureaucrat to approve.

This struck many as draconian overreach into people's private lives. Screw that. They figured that what one did on their own remote parcel out in the middle of nowhere was *their* business.

In striking contrast, the first wave of relatively affluent residents hadn't at all seemed to mind meeting these exhaustive, super-exacting building standards to become legal residents. It was just the way things were done, the price one paid as a responsible citizen. Sure, they probably grumbled, but they'd scrupulously toed the line. The local bureaucracy had perhaps grown accustomed to a public that so dutifully complied with the full letter of the law, and they strove to maintain a tight rein on code enforcement. Maybe, too, they were coming under pressure from the state with its new, comprehensive requirements for new subdivisions, and they tried to do damage control in places that had slipped in under the wire with the old, super-lax regulations.

And possibly some less-than-solid-citizen lot buyers were already dropping anchor — openly or furtively — and living in unconnected trailers, motorhomes and hastily thrown-together shacks. The county felt the need to get tough with such ne'er-do-wells bent on so blatantly disregarding its chiseled-in-stone rules and regulations.

Oh, the camper and the resident should be friends

One story circulated about a respectable lot-owning couple who early on tried to follow the rules but were denied a permit. They'd only wanted to pour a cement slab for their brief annual RV vacation visits, but were told no way. They would first have to install a well and a septic system, and connect to the power supply, before they could pour that slab. Sorry, folks, it doesn't matter if you only visit a few weeks a year; the code's the code.

One suspects that the first wave of dwellers, having themselves gone through that mill, were apprehensive that among the well over 1,000 individual lot owners were bound to be some who'd try end-running the system, refuse to play by the rules and render unto Caesar. If so, their suspicions would soon be justified in spades. They'd pressure the health and building department by immediately reporting every infraction their diligent searches uncovered, expecting a quick response to nip things in the bud.

This, perhaps, was to discourage even above board vacationers like that couple, as they were now effectively intruding on the incipient residential scene as it tenuously coalesced and hoped to maintain the hamlet's compliant building standards. Legal dwellers expected — *demanded* — that local authorities enforce the same letter of the law with which they'd so diligently complied at great expense, time and effort, dammit.

Fair's fair, after all.

However it all came down precisely, attempts at stringent code enforcement on how to live on — apparently, even just visit — your own property out in the middle of nowhere had a predictable way of inspiring more and more to view them as unreasonable rules, deserving of being ignored.

As the Lebanese-American poet and mystic Kahlil Gibran put it in *The Prophet,* "You delight in laying down laws, yet you delight more in breaking them."

When a straggling flock of happy-go-lucky, rebellious back-to-the-landers, many of decidedly modest means (like me, later), entered the scene, stage left, intent on planting themselves on the new parcels before the signature ink on the sales contract had a chance to dry, that's when all hell *really* broke loose in the Vista.

— **CHAPTER 4** —

Snowball's chance

First, there was the outrage from locals and landholding family members over the sale itself, before the place had even *begun* to develop. Then the electrification brouhaha. Now came the explosive reaction to the slowly but surely emerging plague of non-compliant-minded miscreants loosely referred to as hippies. (Or, more commonly, "those *damn* hippies.")

They were determined to settle on the cheap in what the first-comers had come to think of as *their* place, perhaps understandably, given their massive investments and the odds that few other landholders appeared interested in similarly building to code.

The territorial imperative was a powerful force to reckon with.

The Vista's already uber-testy vibe now shifted into overdrive. Dutifully rule-obeying residents, angst-ridden over how their newborn respectable promised land was suddenly facing clear and present danger from young scofflaw lot buyers moving in, went unhinged. A snowball of furious contention rapidly grew to such monstrous proportions that it was as if some demonic force had seized the place and held it in a death grip.

Once I came on board a few years later and sensed the place's wound spirit of contention, I'd eventually wonder if a good dose of squirrelly vibes might've somehow been baked into Vista from its very beginning for some reason. It would help explain the intensity of the off-the-charts meltdown of tolerance and civility unfolding. When I heard from neighbors that the extended Martin family reportedly was furious over the sale of a prized part of their ancestral holdings by one of their own, it was an *aha* moment.

In any event, bitter contention seemed destined to bedevil the would-be peaceful realm for ages. And the sad legacy lingers to this day.

In a nutshell, between

- an embittered farming/ranching community coming to view Vista's inhabitants through distorted fun-house mirrors as a weird, invasive mix of imperious big-city exiles and irascible, dirt-poor hillbillies;

- teeth-gnashing, code-conforming residents on the warpath over the emergence of code-ignoring dwellers wrecking the place's respectability, living standards and property values;

- almost-certain skyrocketing power extension costs putting the kibosh on any further affordable home building;

- disillusioned and resentful absentee parcel holders, many or most indifferent to the day-to-day realities and ongoing needs of its few residents to remain a standard community, feeling stuck with all-but-unbuildable lots they could no longer enjoy or sell without losing their shirts;

- non-conforming residents, taking heat from the aforementioned frothing-at-the-mouth firstcomers and kicking back hard, defying a system they viewed as oppressive; and

- put-upon county authorities over time essentially giving up even *trying* to enforce the building code in a place locals hadn't wanted and that seemed to exist only for outsiders…

…between all these, the place never had (you knew it was coming) a snowball's chance in hell.

A querulous spirit of dizzying proportions came to infect the once-tranquil backwoods. A contentious force field hovered over the outwardly appearing serene, high desert woodlands like so many dark storm clouds forever threatening to rain on the parade of everyone — detached speculators, absentee property holders, and code-legal and 'outlaw' dwellers alike.

No matter how many residents might dedicate themselves to trying to turn the place around over the years and salvage the seemingly once-promising development, it would never rise above being a stalled-out, for all practical purposes, primitive recreational resort that had tried to be something more and failed. A soured-investment boondoggle. A "ghost subdivision." One that had so spectacularly failed to grow into (and remain) a viable, functional standard community that its potential appeared arrested, tried and convicted for life without the possibility of parole.

In realtors' stark insider parlance, the place was roadkill.

—◦◦⟨✕⟩◦◦—

'It hasta be Shasta'

But for anyone on a super-tight budget, who wanted to get back to the land and wasn't overly picky, the generously sized, affordable parcels, so close to the monarchal mountain and going begging, appeared as a gift from heaven.

In 1978, I was between homes, as the expression goes, squatting on land in the Emigrant Wilderness near Sonora, north of Yosemite. By living frugally for several months in warm weather, I'd managed to save up a good portion of the SSI disability checks I received at the time, hoping to accrue enough to buy a small piece of land somewhere and, over time, construct a modest country home. I'd been more homeless than not for seven years, and, alas, was essentially clueless about how to support myself without some help from the government.

I'd just gotten word back from a Yreka realtor I'd contacted at Strout Realty confirming that several good-sized parcels were still available in Mt. Shasta Vista at refreshingly affordable prices. I went to sleep happily that night, sure that my course was set. I would move to the base of the big rock candy mountain, whose image I fondly remember gazing at as a child on the souvenir Dunsmuir window decal on our family's 1950 Plymouth Woody during long road trips, and whose likeness adorned the countless 13-cent Shasta Cola's cream sodas I slurped down growing up in San Francisco. Its catchy slogan had always tickled me: "It hasta be Shasta."

Perhaps as if to show there was no doubt whatsoever that my future course was locked in, the universe sent me a confirmation during sleep that night. It lasted only an instant, but it was easily the most fantastic dream I've ever had. In it, multiple images of Mt. Shasta kaleidoscopically swam around in circles, big as life, while out of the middle came the triumphal voices of Peter, Paul and Mary merrily singing "This Land is Your Land."

Down the rabbit hole

Preceding my own arrival by years, the more free-wheeling, non-compliant dwellers invading the once upright and reputable domain were busy jumping down rabbit holes into their own private worlds that the realm's rarefied energies could so easily foster. Soon enjoying wild Mad Hatter tea parties all but oblivious to the outside world and its bothersome rules and regulations, ignored with pirates' glee, they dismissed as largely impotent the ravings of the Queen of Hearts, in the guise of a largely powerless property owners' board and its minions, who were now essentially screaming, "They'll build to code or it's off with their heads!"

Expanding on *Alice's Adventures in Wonderland* analogies a bit more: Standing in for the mischievous Cheshire Cat was the spirit of social rebellion afoot, eschewing the dull acceptance of prevailing, sometimes overstrict law-and-order norms. And the hookah-smoking caterpillar? None other than the stony, spiraling vortex energies of massive Mount Shasta itself, the backwoods development clinging to its foothills a half hour away from any town's modifying influence, so much under its surreality-inducing sway that it seemed to ask of anyone venturing into its dreamy, cockeyed realm, "Who are *you?*"

Planetary crown chakra?

According to one definition of vortex energy, offered by Ashalyn, founder of a local outfit, Shasta Vortex Adventures, which encourages the exploration and embrace of the region's metaphysical energies for spiritual growth:

"A vortex is a confluence or coming together of planetary ley lines and guidelines. As these lines meet, they create a spiraling motion, which can swirl down into the earth, up into the cosmos, or move in both directions at the same time. This movement increases the vibrational frequency of that area, making it easier to connect with the realms of spirit."

Some new age thinkers believe that Mount Shasta is no less than, variously, the root or crown chakra of the entire planet. Others say Mount Kailash in Tibet, "the roof of the world," is the crown chakra; and Sedona, Arizona, or Machu Picchu, Peru, or the Scottish Highlands is its root chakra. But everyone at least agrees that Shasta definitely emanates a subtle, powerful and mysterious force. One that affects everyone within its field — and perhaps not always in a good way if one's individual upper chakra circuits are clogged.

Whether the Vista was in an actual energy vortex or not, being under the mountain's sway could definitely induce some wild fantasies, if not outright hallucinations. A guest at my place from Montreal once got ecstatic when he thought he was seeing UFOs in the distance at night, moving slowly in opposite directions across the mountain's flanks; it was the headlights of nighttime traffic on State Highway 97. Add to this the fact that it's such an untamed land, and it could easily erase from mind any bothersome notions of following a fading social order's often wearisome, unduly restrictive and arbitrary ways.

It wouldn't begin to describe their unbridled fury to say code-compliant residents were merely upset when the quasi-anarchic scene ignited. But, happening in almost spontaneous combustion, it was perhaps not unlike their own scrambling, jumbling arrival and *their* seriously upsetting the region's long-time residents. Maybe in a way every newcomer becomes an invader of sorts. In any event, these newcomers were *definitely* not their kind. The fledgling upscale-rustic community they'd pinned such great hopes on and poured tons of energy, time, and resources into establishing was in grave peril. As far as their quietly upbeat but buttoned-down, by-the-book, retiring rural lifestyle was concerned, they were facing clear and present danger.

Endangered wonderland

If they didn't mobilize to stem the tide and *demand* that the county rigorously enforce its own friggin' codes with which they themselves had so thoroughly complied, all would be lost, their nascent sweet-spot retirement hamlet gone with the wind. So, at the Queen's behest, they summoned the Card Soldiers in the guise of the county's health and building departments — sometimes accompanied by a deputy, should a situation threaten to be gnarly (and, in time, as a matter of course) — to restore law and order in the now fraught, overwrought wonderland.

Time would, of course, prove their most determined efforts a losing battle in the long run. County authorities would all but abandon residential code enforcement after repeated efforts failed to take hold. And in much later years, a hemorrhaging county budget would lead to the elimination of the enforcement post altogether for a critical half-decade, sounding the death knell for ever regaining a handle on such matters, at least out in the remote Vista "badlands."

Code-compliant residents, stunned by the regional government's seeming growing inability or unwillingness to enforce its own statutes — among those they'd honored and obeyed their whole lives and deemed set in concrete — were left spitting nails mad, bent into pretzels, undies in a bunch, fit to be tied, pick your metaphor.

In short, they wuz *pissed*.

Briefly enjoyed paradise

Despite what had appeared such an auspicious start, first as a de facto shared vacation resort land, then as a nascent rural retirement community, the latter was enjoyed only briefly by the few dozen among the some 1,500 absentee lot owners (allowing for multiple-lot holders), before the place began its inexorable descent into chaos. It became a hopeless oil-and-water mix of respectable code-approved homes and tumbledown trailers, tents, mobile homes, and jerry-built dwellings, thrown together amid a sea of empty parcels compromised for further recreational use and too remote, costly and dicey to build on to code.

A palpable feeling of chronic instability, confusion and contention filled the land. The occasional visit to the still mostly uninhabited regions by diehards hoping to avoid heated politics and still enjoy camping on the more isolated parcels no doubt resulted in mixed experiences.

The place became hopelessly snared between two worlds. Now skitzy in purpose, its reason for being had gotten hazy shortly after its start: What was it, a lingering seasonal campground or a budding year-round community? Either way, it seemed to be an unwanted child, bestowed with little or no support from the county and surrounding community — or, soon enough, even from its own, teeth-gnashing residents. Not to mention the numerous disillusioned investors scattered across the nation.

Newcomers found themselves caught up in the polarization intensifying between the growing code-defiant and the dutifully law-abiding. Residents were like distressed sea voyagers adrift in a lifeboat, left to squabble, bicker and antagonize each other till the cows came home (to mix metaphors). The Vista, frozen in time and nursing a serious identity crisis, appeared deprived of ever finding a rightful place in the sun.

Emboldened by the realm's remoteness

Despite such a crushing load of handicaps, over the years there continued a steady trickle of buyers who were increasingly unconventional. Some wanted to live entirely off-grid and sensed that the place didn't always follow society's sometimes over-restrictive ways, at least not effectively. More and more were intent on immediately moving onto the super-secluded, view-inspiring, irresistibly cheap parcels just as they were: instant Eden.

Beyond the long-term investors feeling stuck with holdings in the arrested development, disinterested speculators still hoping to turn a profit, and the dwindling few who'd yet hoped to continue retreating on their parcels time to time... beyond these was that wild card forever to be reckoned with:

land-hungry people. People, often financially insecure and burned out on the high cost and hassles of city living, who craved natural solitude and peace and quiet.

People drawn to the affordable lots like moths to flame. For the equivalent of a month's town rent, one could cover the down payment on a generously sized piece of remote, wooded land with dazzling mountain view, where one could live and call home once scoring an old trailer or mobile home, or, at the least, camp out in nicer weather.

The place gave such people the opportunity to escape nature-challenged urban living, with its soulless overpriced ticky-tacks and greedy landlords, and live more simply.

They'd cross their fingers and hope to be left alone to dwell between the cracks of society with its costly living standard, which so often made making ends meet next to impossible. While some of us with modest resources grudgingly bit the bullet and slowly built to code, others, blissfully ignorant of, or studiously ignoring, the mundane city-centric regulations trying to be enforced deep in the boonies, had more of a pronounced *Building code? What building code? You're kidding, right?* attitude. One couldn't blame them. People, if they had their druthers, unless masochists, wanted their living scenes to be as simple and carefree as possible.

Encouraging factors

Several factors encouraged the succeeding waves of non-compliant dwellers:

- Again, it was historic times: A tectonic shift in human consciousness and radically changing lifestyles were underway globally; massive numbers wanted to get out of Dodge and back to nature.

- The place was off the beaten path, almost like its own little kingdom, a seemingly charmed outland that felt safely beyond city-centric, restrictive regulations.

- The abandoned — but lingering in spirit — first-generation, camp-use-only vibe had left enough murky uncertainty over what constituted allowable land use to take ready advantage of.

- The county had dwindling success in sustained residential code enforcement, despite having fought and won many of its earliest battles.

Some among the first nonconforming builders — variously labeled code violators, illegal residents and, perhaps the unkindest cut of all, squatters (on their own land, mind you) — moved in with a casual air of "Hey, what's the big deal? We're just building a little shelter on our own parcel here out in the middle of nowhere; c'mon, you can't be serious."

Over time, learning about the place's drawn-out code-conformity war and the increasingly spotty enforcement, some newbies grew bold enough to go on the offensive. They'd pull in their sundry derelict travel trailers and mobile homes, or build ramshackle shelters on the fly, bearing openly defiant, mocking attitude of *Hee, hee, what're you goin' to do about it, huh?*

Others were more like screaming eagles: "Hey, this was still America last time I checked. This is my land, and I'll do whatever I damn well please on it. You'd better back off if you know what's good for you."

CHAPTER 5

A law unto themselves

Living in non-code shelter construction and utilities-bereft, foundationless mobile homes became more and more common. Eventually, it seemed like unapproved structures were popping up like mushrooms after a drenching rain. While some shelters were artful and relatively ambitious, others were bereft of any charm except perhaps to their inhabitants, proud of their handiwork and resourcefulness and psyched to have fulfilled the primal need to build shelters against the elements.

It was almost as though such dwellers had time-warped back to the pioneer era, when plains settlers built primitive, earth-sheltered soddies, and forest settlers threw together rude log cabins. As if, late in the twentieth century, the development had somehow mysteriously become an Old West frontier, unmoored from the time stream. One blissfully removed from the modern era with all its spirit-stifling rules and regulations about how one was *supposed* to live.

Enjoying unapproved structures proved problematic

Though few such dwellings were ever officially "red-tagged" by the county (that is, designated unlawful to inhabit, with ominous official warning notice tacked to the front door), they still carried a powerful stigma. The disapproving, hostile reactions of code-compliant neighbors to the fact that they existed at all could make it a bit problematic to enjoy staying in them with anything approaching peace of mind for all but the thicker-skinned.

Gradually, various legal residents — feeling light years away from any dependable and responsive law enforcement save for more serious matters (even then, a 45-minute wait time wasn't uncommon) — essentially deemed themselves a law unto themselves. Feeling the need to act as citizen deputies, as it were, to keep the rabble at bay and the realm law-abiding, old-guard members patrolled the sprawling backwoods roads like bloodhounds, trying to sniff out reportable health and building code violations and then baying a storm over the phone lines. Some residents, even if they themselves were compliant, found such a rigid obsession with absolute code compliance a real downer. At times it felt downright scary, as if some two-bit fascist regime had surreally risen up in the middle of would-be tranquil lands.

Gnarly incident

Turning this prevailing vigilante tendency on its ear, one non-compliant resident decades later had just taken severe heat over being suspected of growing pot (he wasn't). It was a deed then very much illegal and vigorously prosecuted, with state laws aligned with federal statutes. Penalties included mandatory prison terms of up to three years, possible property confiscation, and fines up to $10,000.

One hot summer day, a sheriff's helicopter swooped in and hovered dangerously close above the giant truck tarp he'd stretched between the trees over his old school bus home to provide critical shade. It started to tear loose. No doubt having been reported as a non-compliant troublemaker, they appeared convinced (or maybe just hopeful) that he was trying to hide a verboten cannabis grow beneath it, so they could make a grand bust and make the place safe again for honest folk. Outraged at the invasion of his airspace and how the chopper's air turbulence was tearing loose his tarp — and by no means shy — he openly flipped them off while offering his darkest scowl. Naturally, they couldn't let this affront to their authority pass. Other sheriff deputies soon barged onto his land, without a warrant, loaded for bear. They pointed assault weapons at him, as if itching for an excuse to open fire.

While seemingly callous and thick-skinned, he was actually sensitive — and a bit of an actor. On the wings of this traumatic incident, he tried displacing some of his angst by riding about on his motorcycle with a prominently visible sidearm and confronting various residents over things he pretended *he* disapproved of.

Buy in haste

No doubt, many of the land buyers interested in actually using the land were at best no more than vaguely aware of the place's sundry handicaps and liabilities, any number of which routinely turned off your more circumspect land shopper exercising due diligence. They were giddy about being able to grab such nice-sized pieces of unspoiled land in such a popular recreational region at such dirt-cheap prices. Eureka! It was practically the modern-day equivalent of history's Forty Acres and a Mule government giveaway (if likewise deemed-marginal land). The lots proved so affordable that any commonly felt need to make a judicious assessment seemed to fly out the window, aided and abetted by the mountain's at times almost otherworldly energy.

Parcels got snapped up like so many bargain basement steals.

Before the place's sundry disheartening realities at last per-colated one's gray matter, the would-be, latter-day pioneers spun all sorts of dreams and schemes about how they'd enjoy their new secluded woodlands, so nicely hidden amid the maze of private country roads, beyond modern times' slings and arrows of outrageous fortune.

Add to these legal and illegal residents the more thoughtful and involved investors who, despite discouraging unfolding developments, stubbornly clung to the notion that the par-cels might still make good retreats and were worthy of maybe someday building homes or cabins on, either for themselves or others they'd sell to after enjoying them a while. Also, add in the many parcel flippers who grabbed the lots, imagining how quickly they'd move them up the food chain as the number of code-legal structures increased, making easy money. Add these together, and the overall property ownership became hopelessly deadlocked in a tangle of wildly conflicting intentions forever at cross purposes.

The result: Mt. Shasta Vista was left in a perpetual state of chaotic confusion.

'Why don't we just move here?'

The first-generation settlers at first might have seemed no more than adventurous vacationing campers wanting to kick back in nature for a while in their own private campgrounds. But even as they relished being on the land, willing to make generous allowances for the notable lack of infrastructure — maybe even embracing it — some, again, had no doubt been sussing the place's possibilities all along for maybe building retirement residences.

While such a lack of infrastructure and the absence of formal plans had presented little or no problem during the first years of sole camp and retreat use — trailers being self-contained and one otherwise resigned to making like a bear in the woods a while — the situation would, of course, become the place's Achilles' heel. Years after having built their approved residences, resource-shy and instant-home-seeking others would roll the dice and drop anchor, wanting no one's approval but their own for how they chose to live.

Consequently, over the decades, as the Vista morphed from primitive camping ground to ephemeral, fledgling retiree rural community to mongrel, anything-goes outback, it became the wayward realm the county eventually threw up its hands at in exasperation and dumbfounded bewilderment. It seemed as if they'd allowed some dread Frankenland to be created that was now threatening the villagers by its presence; it served as a constant thorn in the county authorities' side.

They were at a loss over how to stem the apparent anarchy and lawlessness emerging amid the thin scattering of approved homes. Some, maybe eventually most, took refuge in magical thinking, imagining the whole place simply disappearing. Being in such a remote location made this relatively easy: out of sight, out of mind.

The onerous building code vs. the owner-builder

Consequently, unsanctioned shelters multiplied. More and more, it seemed lot buyers eager to settle lacked the funds or the willingness to build to code or both. Freer spirits, again, considered the exacting codes needlessly complicated, insultingly intrusive and ridiculously expensive to comply with. They felt such codes only reflected the cushy standard of living of the more affluent strata of society, and that they were being forced on others of lesser means to keep them under their thumb.

One might've concluded that in a way it was America's own caste system — an economic one, with rigid insistence that everyone dance to the tune of the more affluent… or they'd be treated like effluent.

But hoping to avoid such stringent codes — and the inflated lifestyles of would-be upward mobiles, many of them attempting to live beyond their means and soon drowning in debt — was the very reason so many moved out to the Vista in the first place: to get back to basics, to live more simply, in closer harmony with nature, within one's means. Of course, some were doubtless thinking short-term, intending to stay only as long as they could before attracting too much attention to their non-copacetic shelters from uptight busybody neighbors who would rat them out to the authorities.

The way of thinking of your more reasonable person was that it was one thing to maybe have a few commonsense ordinances in place to prevent unsightly, flimsy owner-built structures that might blow over in the first strong wind, and to ensure critical hygienic standards for the sake of public health and safety. But it was another entirely to demand that one living on their own land out in the middle of nowhere be made to construct a home for themselves needing a continuous, massive foundation, being at least a minimum size, overbuilding by a safety factor of five, installing double-glazed windows, super-insulating the roof, wiring and plumbing the entire structure, installing a fire sprinkler system...

Somewhere along the line, there appeared a disconnect from reasonableness.

Trying to relax the code

During the 1970s, a grassroots effort emerged led by a group of outraged rural owner-builders in Mendocino County, California. As brought out in the 1976 book, *The Owner-Builder and the Code: Politics of Building Your Home,* by Ken Kern, they'd been evicted for code violations from their handmade crackerbox palaces on private land in the dead of winter. They and their supporters rallied for the state legislature to establish less onerous building requirements for anyone building dwellings on their own land. It led to then-governor Jerry Brown approving a Class K housing bill specifically aimed at easing building requirements for such rural owner-builders. But by 1981, the bill had been so watered down by an apparently construction-industry-friendly state assembly that it was left to each county to decide whether to adopt it.

Only three did. Vista's Siskiyou, not always the most progressive-minded county, wasn't one. Its building department, at home in dealing with contractors who knew the drill in their sleep, appeared hostile or at least wary and uncomfortable with owner-builders. They didn't want to waste their time guiding first-time builders through the myriad steps required to navigate the maze of regulations and specifications they were paid to enforce. "If you can't understand it, hire a contractor" was their dismissive attitude. They assumed — not without reason, given the code's incredibly far-reaching and pricey requirements — that many owner-builders would try to "cheat" the code at every given opportunity.

'Did we ever sign you off?'

Over a decade after getting my own tiny house green-tagged (despite having indeed fudged on a few minor specs, while exceeding code on others), I ran into Mr. Fiock, the by-then-retired head building inspector, at the Yreka post office. He had come out once, at the start, no doubt to strike the fear of God into me to knuckle under and obey Caesar's edicts. Perhaps intuiting I hadn't fully toed the line and still wanting to take me to task, he furrowed his brow and asked doubtfully, "Did we ever sign you off?" (My strategy all along had been to keep calling them up and bugging them with questions on their endless specifications, to the point they finally got so exasperated, they were all, "Just build the damn thing and leave us alone.")

While such draconian requirements no doubt discouraged many earlier would-be non-compliant builders, over time, as the once-iron grip of regulatory bureaucracy's enforcement relaxed, a rebellious spirit gained ground. People aspired to build rural shelters on their own land however they fancied, thank you, never thinking to get any *Mother-may-I?* permission from some obscure, meddling bureaucratic authority and, adding insult to injury, have to pay for the privilege. Though on a much smaller scale, playing "Beat the building code" became as popular a cat-and-mouse game as the *What pot laws?* mindset of much later times. Bound and determined to live on their bought-and-paid-for properties, many Vistans figured possession was nine-tenths of the law. Their headspace was, again, "Hey, this is my own private property, and I'll do whatever I damn well please on it; go jump in a lake if you don't like it."

Regret at leisure

As the place's long-festering problems became all too clear to parcel owners, a complex, intense love-hate relationship with the land emerged. Especially among those who'd hoped to settle on their lots long-term and enjoy long-sought solitude. It was, "Buy in haste, regret at leisure." Over the years it became a sad, familiar song. Lured by the rural development's afford-able remote parcels with what at first *appeared* a refreshing absence of any "Thou Shalt" authority — leastwise one with any teeth — more than a few buyers tuned out the snarling posted signs as little more than ineffectual, blustery Barney Fife bluff.

But then, any buyer who leaned toward being at least nominally law-abiding was disheartened to realize that the signs sometimes meant business. If one wanted to make use of the place beyond camping for up to 30 days a year and not risk the rug suddenly getting yanked out from under one's feet, or at least always feel under duress, the lots' woeful lack of infrastructure required shelling out a small fortune to get things squared away.

It was like ten-cent parcels had a hidden million-dollar spoiler attached.

For the same or related reasons, the lots became an albatross about the necks of investors, speculators and would-be vacationers alike. With holdings no longer part of a simple, virtual recreational development once homes, power and phone lines began cluttering the once semi-pristine landscape, they could no longer sell them at a profit as either private camping property or desirable building sites… at least, not to anyone who knew the score and was convention-minded. And that didn't take much sussing to discover. One had only to talk to your typical walking-wounded, teeth-gnashing resident. Their ears would soon be singed by the aggrieved party, who, warming to their task, raked the place over the coals with almost demonic intensity.

It was a buyer's remorse destined to become a pattern in countless owners' relationships with the singular land that, strange to say, often felt at once both blessed and cursed.

But the seductive lure of the affordable backwoods parcels under the protective presence of the big rock candy mountain, feeling worlds away from noisy, overwound city living, kept grabbing would-be residents and impulsive investors alike.

While the latter only thought to flip the obviously undervalued parcels, a growing number of the former settled in and tried ignoring mundane concerns like code compliance, until, out of the blue, it bit them on the backside and they joined the howling chorus of grievously disenchanted.

CHAPTER 6

Lots practically sold themselves

While the lots were technically zoned for single-family residential development, they were first marketed primarily as recreational land. Maybe over time owners would get together and grow it into something more, maybe not. The lack of any residential development plan from the outset led to a strong inertia that kept the energy stuck. The parcels seemed to hold no higher ambition than to serve as primitive camping retreats unless one had the resources to conform to rigorous code and supply all one's own needed infrastructure. And was of course one enamored by the thought of living so far off the beaten path.

As I've speculated, some who had fully conformed might not have been all that community-minded. Or at least they'd cease to be once things got dicey and their happy bubble of an exclusive, tight-knit retirement enclave burst, leaving them feeling surrounded by a bunch of nonconforming yahoos. They might've never given a hoot if the place grew or not. Maybe they even *hoped* it wouldn't — more seclusion for them, no immediate neighbors beyond those they already knew to have to deal with.

While the bare-bones development was all upfront and legal under existing lax California laws covering rural subdivisions, informed developers must have known something was in the wind. Soon new legislation would require new starts to supply all supporting infrastructure. It had been the last chance to make a fast buck with minimal outlay by rolling out such recreational-property subdivisions that offered no amenities beyond simple road access and whatever features Mother Nature might see fit to provide.

Overambitious

Developer Collins must have decided he needn't risk investing any more time, money, or effort in the project to move the lots than he did. Playing the market and perhaps being a bit over-optimistic with the sprawling size of the development, he apparently lacked the certainty that a standard residential community could ever flourish here. If so, time seemed to prove his hunch. While it appeared enthusiasm over the chance to wing it and spend a little time now and then amid the solitude of one's own bit of woodlands, serene Mt. Shasta watching over big as life, had proven contagious, there appeared to be a striking lack of interest, apart from a tiny handful of back-to-the-land lot holders, to ever want to actually *live* here.

Then again, maybe it was all a self-fulfilling prophecy.

In any case, with a bit of sizzling ad copy, the lots practically sold themselves. It was the cheap speculation of tangible property; the parcels always held some vague promise of someday, somehow, proving to be useful. Being so affordable yet having such an inspiring view of the mountain made snapping up the parcels irresistible, a nice little bauble to add to one's investment portfolio.

After springing for drilling test wells and buying an existing well having an impressive replenishment rate, just off Vista land, to satisfy the county that there was indeed water, Collins must've been hopeful every part of the elevation-varied realm might provide enough water should owners ever want to settle on their parcels. Or even if they just wanted to visit and have their own well. But he might have downplayed the depth of the water table in the higher elevations in Section 13 and, especially, Section 23. Instead, he painted a happy picture of the unofficial de facto community well that every lot owner was of course more than welcome to use.

At least it's a nice retreat

Bottom line: He'd created at the least a simple, collectively owned semi-wilderness retreat realm in a popular vacation region — one with the potential to, however unlikely, become something more in a way that might benefit all property hold-ers. Not just a few who could afford the excessive costs involved in getting code-compliant.

For what it was worth, in the first years each lot enjoyed immaculately well-maintained road access and was platted to a fare-thee-well, with corner boundaries marked off by short, soon-rusted red steel pipes and ribboned lathe sticks with exact, scrawled bearings. Nearly 90% offered varying degrees of views of the mountain, some breathtaking. Who needed anything more? In those giddy times of renewed awareness of life's possibilities, it was a perfect whatever-it-was just the way it was, a dreamland of one's imagination that needn't conform to any pesky mundane waking realities.

But with the real estate game the way it was, the spiel and cheap prices also attracted many who had no foreseeable plans to ever camp *or* build. They were almost certainly the overwhelming majority among the some 1,500 initial parcel buyers. They'd snap them up as long-term investments or short-term speculations, happy to get in on the ground floor of what might prove a sure thing. They imagined others — not them, thank you — soon clamoring to camp on the lots or build homes and vacation cabins, both scenarios that would nicely drive up land values.

Now what do we do with it?

Yet others, though primarily speculating, might've sampled their untamed properties a time or two, curious to discover what it was they'd bought sight unseen. No doubt some had never owned land before and were excited just to have it, but were unsure what to do with it. The land and its inspiring mountain view might've grabbed some once they camped on it, and they decided to hold onto the lots long term. Again, some buyers surely must've flirted with the idea of building dwellings if and when things progressed enough to enjoy visiting and living in them for a while, before selling once the novelty of Vista living wore thin.

So many Americans, restless, rootless, and periodically on the move, appeared to always view their current shelter as an investment, first and foremost. The notion of ever dropping anchor and cultivating a long-term residence anywhere, at least before reaching retirement age, if even then, was seldom considered.

Giant monkey wrench in the works

I'd guesstimate that no more than 10% of lot owners kept entertaining the idea of building for any reason once the campaign to electrify the entire place failed and ignited a major falling-out among lot holders. It had thrown a monkey wrench in the works, creating ill will and a pronounced disenchantment with the place and its prospects. Some degree of cohesive group vision and a willingness to work together in a common cause had been needed if the place ever hoped to serve the long-term interests of a majority of the diverse group of some 1,500 lot holders.

It appeared that there was now little, if any, vision left to be had for love or money.

The bold dream of the few who'd gone for the gusto and made their former campgrounds their new home was cramped by disappointed lot holders who bore only a detached financial interest in the place. They were dead weight, dragging on efforts to ever solidify the incipient settlement. This they did by voting down any special assessment proposal to generate improvements.

But doggone it, everything had just seemed so peachy keen and hunky dory at first. Jazzed new rural landowners viewed the place and its promise through rose-colored glasses. They were blissfully ignorant of the festering behind-the-scenes storm clouds brewing over the place's very existence, of locals' cantankerous resentment toward the bunch of high-and-mighty city folks crowding in, dripping with cash and taking over their backwoods stomping grounds, upsetting a long-established rural way of life.

Keep them doggies movin'

Even into the early eighties, local ranchers seasonally led sporadic cattle drives along short stretches of Vista's frontage of County Highway A-12 between grazing areas. The road had a cattle grate (very noisy when driven over; the clanking sound was heard a mile away). For generations, the region had been a sprawling cattle land owned by the Martins. One got the feeling they enjoyed pretending the occasional impatient vehicle traffic wasn't even there, that, it being in their genes, they'd time-warped back to the pre-auto 1800s Western frontier era, when the entire region was their own rugged kingdom. *Git along, little doggies.*

Over the following years, newer lot owners could fail to realize how seriously the county — once lot owners started building in the often-rocky volcanic foothills and struggling with water and eventually blowing off code compliance — regretted having ever okayed the blasted place. How they came to view the forlorn development as a lemon vehicle they'd bought against their better judgment and were stuck with. How they forever cast a jaundiced eye towards the realty misfire and its bickering residents with a rueful, *what-the-hell-did-we-ever-approve* remorse and sometimes even hard-bitten disgust.

Idyllic camping

With no such distressing undercurrents apparent at first, the earliest nature-hungry city vacationers had felt free to enjoy their idyllic backwoods enclave with the prevailing lighthearted spirit of the times that often bordered on outright euphoria. One had the convenience and luxury of camping on their very own piece of secluded, scenic land for up to 30 days a year, rather than, say, pay daily to chance camping some place where others were setting up 20 feet away with a passel full of squalling kids.

The majority of original parcel owners, again, hailed from the smog-choked Los Angeles region, where the developer was based and launched his marketing campaign; others were from the Bay Area and the Central Valley. Purchasers pitched tents or rolled in travel trailers and RVs to savor the serenity and drink in the clean mountain air and inspiring eponymous Mt. Shasta vista, the mountain *right there*, practically in their own front yard.

The terrain was known as high desert woodlands: high, dry, and wooded. Though powerful seasonal windstorms often proved treacherous and unnerving — roaring through like a runaway freight, due to the massive mountain displacing and condensing stormy air currents in a Venturi effect — the place, like nearby Lake Shastina and Juniper Valley, otherwise often enjoyed an enviable banana-belt climate. Summers were typi-cally hot and bone-dry, but there were plenty of juniper trees and, on a few parcels, scattered pine, to provide welcome shade. Some years saw a summer thunderstorm or two to cool things down a while. Those in the northwest end of the Vista were a short hike away from Lake Shastina's remote cross-country irrigation canal to take refreshing dips in. And the mountain's spectacular northwestern, glacier-clad side did wonders keeping one feeling cooler just by gazing on its chilled splendor.

'Bye 'n' bye' came fast

Significantly, developer Collins had casually hinted early on how the place might make a dandy place to "retire to bye 'n' bye." He appeared to be responding to a growing enthusiasm among his fellow repeat vacationing campers for this very notion. But then again, maybe he'd had it in mind all along — evidenced by his having gotten the lots rezoned for residential use at formation — and was now only deftly orchestrating owners' growing excitement over the idea like a maestro. In any event, he intimated the idea in the official newsletter periodically sent to property owners and avidly read by the small segment of co-owners who enjoyed coming each year to their new, very own semi-wilderness outpost. Dozens responded, but probably most were only the repeat vacationers who already had the idea firmly in mind.

However it went, being located at the central top of the Golden State, Mount Shasta its regal crown, made it nearly impossible for nature lovers *not* to be smitten by the low-key charm of the realm. Enough to go for it and indeed retire here to live on their often-secluded parcels year-round, or even before retirement and then split time between residences.

Since practically next-door Lake Shastina was springing up, initially as a second-home vacation community, along with several other regional rural subdivisions, bye 'n' bye came fast. It gave the handful of so-minded Vistan landholders the impetus to follow suit, but with a twist: building structures not as second homes but, as Collins had suggested, as full-on retirement residences.

Enviable climate, minus the windstorms

Like Lake Shastina, Mt. Shasta Vista usually received far less snowfall than nearby Weed or the City of Mt. Shasta, offering an attractive climate minus the occasional severe windstorms. This was due to the region's phenomenal crazy-quilt of micro-climates, again, the mountain's doing. Usually, there was just enough powder to enjoy a winter wonderland now and then without getting a sore back shoveling snow, or frostbitten hands putting on chains to get out beyond the then-never-plowed roads.

Long ago the place had tried plowing its roads after one of its rare (then maybe once a decade) heavy snowfalls of 18 to 24 inches; the equipment's blade tore up the cinder road-beds so severely that it required expensive regrading, making it impractical. Thereafter, for decades, until the unusually heavy February 2025 snowstorm hit, by which time the place had worlds more residents, everyone was on their own. (In my 47 years here, I've been snowbound twice, once for a week, once for 11 days.)

Con su permiso:
dealing with an exacting building code

It was understood that, after passing a perc test, each would-be resident was responsible for drilling an approved well, installing an approved septic system and having power lines extended, before becoming eligible to apply for a building permit. Then, only after the application was approved did one have a legal right to live on the land for more than 30 days a year. But, crazy world, once the permit *was* issued, you could live in any structure you wanted — be it trailer, shack or hole in the ground — since it would ostensibly serve as a temporary on-site work shelter during construction.

While building was expected to proceed "in a timely manner," many, unlike feverishly paced contractors, were far from being in a hurry; they could make quite a leisurely effort of things. I stretched out my own home-building period to 42 months while living in a semi-underground, ramshackle 8-by-12-foot hobbit home, which was most decidedly non-code. It tickled me how the building inspector cast a wary eye at it every time he strode by to check the latest construction beyond it; no doubt he had to suppress an urge to red-tag it on the spot.

Once a structure was completed and signed off, the post office assigned a legal street address (or, actually, released an already existing number assigned long ago to every recorded parcel in the county), thereby enabling one to receive mail at the blacktop entrance boxes. Such an address was also ostensibly required to obtain a state driver's license, register to vote, or qualify for FedEx, UPS and OffTrak (or is it OnTrak?) home delivery.

As one might suspect, the extensive health and building codes included endlessly detailed particulars about *everything*: foundation; precise framing method; itemization down to the grade and variety of lumber and kind, size and spacing of every fastener; thorough electrification; exact insulation specs; complete kitchen facilities; indoor plumbing; minimum water pressure… Any unconventional design like a geodome, earthship, cob house or earth-sheltered abode required hiring a qualified engineer to certify that the submitted plan was structurally sound, and one still had to meet all other general specs.

I'd wanted to build a free-form earth-sheltered home, but realized it would cost more and prove a complete disappointment, given the compromises I would've had to make to satisfy rigid code requirements. When an office inspector talked about maybe lowering pre-stressed concrete slabs into the ground by crane to meet strength and insulation requirements, that's when I gave up on that dream.

Building codes were first aimed only at crowded cities

Although the Uniform Building Code had been in place in the U.S. since 1915, enforcement was no doubt relaxed or nonexistent for decades in rural regions. Focus originally had been on crowded cities with their close-packed structures built by detached contractors who'd never live in their creations, and who were tempted to take shortcuts on building integrity, resulting in shoddy construction and sometimes tragedy for the eventual inhabitants. As the founder of the UBC, Rudolf Miller, himself stated early on, he never envisioned the new regulations being applied to rural owner-builders:

"…[W]hen buildings are comparatively small, are far apart, and their use is limited to the owners and builders of them so that, in case of failure of any kind that is not a source of danger to others, *no necessity for building restriction would exist* [italics added]."

His reasonable, commonsense view was obviously abandoned as living densities increased and the government's bureaucratic, power-hungry regulatory powers grew exponentially, alongside higher standards of living and an increase in the complexities of modern living.

But for a long while country landowners could pretty much build cabins and cottages to suit themselves, at their leisure, maybe even play it by ear with the overall design perhaps emerging only halfway through, if even then. It was *their* land, after all, so they could build whatever they blame-well pleased on it. But with bureaucratic regulations' inexorable tendency to become adopted by ever-greater numbers over time (some might say spreading like a cancer), until at last universalized, government authorities began insisting that the same exhaustive guidelines demanded to be adhered to in teeming cities by indifferent contractors, churning out cookie-cutter abodes for others to inhabit, be followed by owner-builders living deep in the boonies on their own remote land.

Of course, if the occupant later sold the place to another, that's when things could get complicated. This was no doubt the rationale behind universalizing building codes: to ensure that a minimum level of comfort, hygiene and safety standards existed in a living structure no matter who built it, where it was located or who occupied it at any given time. And, perhaps more importantly, at least to the powers that be, to ensure that any lending institution floating loans for home construction or property purchases on which structures were built had a salable commodity to recover its investment should the borrower default.

It was having such perceived-as-oppressive ordinances in place in the Vista (and no fine-empowered board of directors to keep a practical carrot-and-stick handle on matters) that led to the growing erosion of respect for specific areas of law and ordinance. At least, by its more nonconformist — sometimes only desperate and cash-trapped — inhabitants of the charm-rich but water- and electricity-poor land.

CHAPTER 7

'Priced to move!'

At its launch, parcels were indeed priced to move. I recall reading in the *Vistascope* newsletter archives how they went for between $750 and $975 each. Prices varied according to parcel size, location, terrain and views. The developer had relatively low overhead and was by no means out to get rich off the project, as he was already successful from past urban development ventures and so could afford to be generous with this special land project. He appeared to hold a genuine affection for the land and the buyers he met while camping during the first few summers. He may have wanted the lot sales to feel like the feel-good bargains they were — or seemed to be.

These prices were 1968 dollars. Adjusting for inflation, that'd be nearly 10 times more in 2025 dollars — about $9,000 — still relatively cheap for such a good-sized chunk of secluded and scenic land, even without water or electricity. The price of undeveloped lots rose for many years after 2015, but then fell after 2022 to $10,000. This restored the constant market value to its level when the place launched 57 years earlier after adjusting for inflation.

'Hey, they're not making any more land'

Initially, there were few infrastructure costs beyond putting in the 66 miles of red cinder roads (many of the main arteries were traced over preexisting logging, livestock-tending and hunting/camping/partying roads); surveying and marking off parcel boundaries; erecting entrance and section corner signs; and planting the first-generation, short wooden 4 x 4 road sign posts, many soon camouflaged by the fast-growing sagebrush wanting to reclaim the land.

First-generation buyers purchased the lots for different reasons — but, again, countless grabbed them out of pure speculation: "Hey, they're not making any more land." Many, no doubt, never even set foot on them, let alone camped on them. Though a handful were indeed excited at the prospect of having their own private campgrounds and entertained thoughts of maybe someday building homes or vacation cabins, arguably the overwhelming majority were only betting on the place and the actions of others… hopefully a good number of others.

Turnkey camp sites?

They anticipated making out like bandits once the place gained in popularity. Maybe it'd grow into a giant, KOA-style camp village, loaded with amenities and services, attracting a flood of campers tickled to have their own recreational properties nestled by Mount Shasta. Perhaps eventually they'd launch time-shares for more improved and secluded camp lots, offering turnkey camping that would later be known as glamping.

However, the place instead evolved into a sparsely populated, briefly standard-grade community. One that might've actually succeeded and endured, maybe indeed driving up parcel values, had every future would-be resident taken responsibility for meeting their own infrastructure needs and built to code, as had all among the first wave of transplants (and as is, of course, almost always the case in more populated areas with any new development).

Obviously, they hadn't. Oftentimes, it seemed that the only reason so many moved in after them was that it offered a cheap place to live in the country for as long as they could keep building code enforcement at bay. And so fortune passed the place by. *Seriously* passed it by.

Counterintuitive

Pouring substantial investments into such primitive, low-cost land felt counterintuitive. Something maybe considered only by a certain people reaching retirement age, flush with cash and bewitched by the land they'd discovered during a euphoric time, and who were primed to collectively transform it into their own year-round, tight-wound Eden. (Plus, again, any with similar cash to plow into building, or the willingness to assume a then far-stricter credit-card debt.)

And, unless a contractor or hiring one, having the disposition, fortitude and determination to deal with the niggling, hoop-jumping, monumentally exasperating process of meeting the code requirements demanded of an owner-builder working under the eagle eye of the building department without going nuts.

Understandably, such a vision and the high cost to meet it didn't elicit ringing endorsements from the less solvent parcel buyers — most of whom would move onto their new lots in a twinkling. ("Hey, why else buy them?") They had maybe only enough to cover the modest down, score an old trailer, throw up a makeshift shelter on the fly from scrap materials or make a small lumberyard splurge and call it okie dokie.

Vestiges of Vista's primitive camping origin linger to this day

It seemed that cheap land and cheap building aspirations really could go together. Since the lots were initially used as de facto primitive camp parcels and later their standard development was hindered by difficult access to water, rocky terrain and distant power lines, the place essentially froze in time. It seemed impossible to ever fully erase the place's primitive, recreation-al-use-only beginnings: *it appeared to be permanently embedded in every last parcel — some 1,550, or 95% — that was officially left undeveloped.*

Earliest investors and speculators likely hadn't considered the possibility of such a wrinkle ever cropping up on top of the high cost of building to code and sinking deep wells. How an epidemic of non-compliant structures, and at times questionable land use, might, almost overnight, drastically erode their holdings' sellability and desirability as places to either camp *or* build on for anyone convention minded. After learning about the few dozen full-on, code-legal homes emerging and hearing developer Collins paint a rosy picture of the place's bright future, they'd assumed everyone would naturally continue building to code.

Misled thinking

Significantly, many speculators, on hearing of the momentous building plans of what turned out to be only a relative few, were almost certainly misled into thinking that there were far more property holders gung-ho on creating an accepted rural community than ever existed. No doubt they'd started salivating like Pavlovian dogs, anticipating the place perhaps following nearby Lake Shastina's lead and building out in a giddy, mad scramble, their bargain lots, soon commanding hefty prices.

Congratulating themselves on having gotten in on the ground floor of what they thought promised to be an easy slam-dunk moneymaker, given time, parcel investors sat back and waited for things to take their merry course. Some would eventually join in and likewise build on their lots, thinking to live in their structures a while before selling and making even greater profits. Or they'd become likewise enamored by the land and, resonating with the retired dwellers' buttoned-down, albeit engaging, bonhomie, decide to stay. But most, having little to no interest in the day-to-day realities of the place's eventual widely scattered residents — or in the vital need to prevent the proliferation of non-code structures and ensuing erosion of property values and livability — couldn't be bothered to even see the dots, let alone connect them. Clueless, they twiddled their thumbs and bided their time. They patiently waited for the parcel values to take off like so many race cars in the Indy 500.

Time-machine boom

They'd only have to wait half a century.

Then, in 2015, nearly three generations after the place's founding, floundering and foundering in another era, parcel prices began an astonishing, dizzying flight to the moon.

Long-depressed values of myriad unimproved lots soared practically overnight. And kept climbing, from going begging at $5,000 to over $150,000 by 2021 amid bidding wars. This was, of course, the result of a double whammy: a national red-hot realty market coinciding with the place's discovery by a flood of emboldened growers who anticipated California legalization of recreational pot and what would prove to be — perhaps predictably, given the modern-day gold rush of intrepid entrepreneurs inundating the land — a flurry of new, untested and, so, hard-to-enforce regulations.

Among the legion of new illicit scaled cannabis patches suddenly proliferating the state, were, besides generations-old white European American growers, recent immigrants and nationals of Russia, Mexico, Armenia, Bulgaria and Montenegro. In Vista's case, those who would snap up the long-fallow parcels by the hundred happened to be largely Asian American and predominantly Hmong (silent "H").

Suddenly, a *growers'* Shangri-la

The new wave of lot holders would also purchase the majority of existing code-conforming homes, as owners lost heart over the drastic changes swamping the place, but were at least mollified by the healthy sale prices the homes suddenly commanded. In short order, the new Vistans would spark a phenomenal transformation into the place becoming a *growers'* Shangri-la. The realtors might just as well have advertised the parcels as:

"Lotus land, for sale cheap. Special realm to pursue wildest dreams in and get rich quick. No reality down."

Okay, maybe that's getting a bit silly. But the new California cannabis statutes would decriminalize unsanctioned commercial grows from a criminal felony down to a civil misdemeanor in most cases, making irresistible the urge to gamble and produce seas of green for an insatiable nationwide underground market. (Maybe it was the legislators who were in lotus land for thinking the new statutes could ever be effectively enforced the way they were written.)

This was the reason — beyond the state being renowned for cultivating high-quality cannabis and having a solid, long-established underground market — for attracting so many, er... *casual* growers. New state laws would leave it to each of the 58 counties to decide whether to allow regulated commercial grows in its unincorporated areas (that is, everywhere beyond city limits, while incorporated cities could vote for dispensaries and regulated commercial grows). Conservative Siskiyou County, with a prevailing *Reefer Madness* mindset, would decline, along with many other counties. But then it would suffer towns like Weed and Mt. Shasta voting in pot dispensaries and regulated grows.

Here was the grand enticement for unlicensed growers: If enough people scaled up unsanctioned cannabis production, then effectively enforcing the restrictions, beyond a bust here and there, often picking the easiest, lowest-hanging fruit, was bound to prove a losing game.

A Dr. Jekyll and Mr. Hyde sort of place

As a result, from 2015 onward, Vista lots began selling like crazy for reasons totally unrelated to infrastructure build-up, still almost nil; new formal development plans, still nonexistent; or, for more than a few who had sunk roots, being a place where one might want to settle long term.

Especially after the widely shared fantasy vision, compliments of that perpetual fantasy inducer, Mount Shasta, of building up a thriving, quixotic, proscribed-grow-based community, faced the chilly winds of reality. Once again, the at-first-seeming idyllic land would suddenly turn gnarly, in something akin to a Dr. Jekyll and Mr. Hyde transformation, as decidedly unpleasant, sporadic eradication campaigns by scrambling authorities, never-say-die, slogged on year after year.

The startling real estate boom, while dumbfounding many, including me, proved only in keeping with Mt. Shasta Vista's perpetual boom-bust nature.

Its cycles might be likened to a bone-dry desert that experienced a brief flash flood once every decade or so. A deluge of land-hungry would-be country squires, bold, unlicensed pot entrepreneurs and cagey speculators periodically rained down on the region, driving up depressed prices on the problematic parcels or trying to. Then, invariably, as things didn't pan out, market values fell back to their default bone-dry level, softer than sponge cake.

Some might've concluded that it was a strange and wild volcanic land that simply refused to be tamed. It was too challenging a place to make a permanent home beyond the few who, for some odd reason, *liked* living out in the middle of nowhere.

Land, ho!

According to the archived copy of the *Vistascope* newsletter sent to lot holders after the project's launch, every lot got snapped up within 18 months.

This fact belies a later common assumption, even among newspaper reporters, that the developer had been left with parcels no one wanted. People wanted them, all right — or *thought* they did, at first. The lots had sold like crazy. It was only later that the hundreds of absentee owners and those they'd sold the lots to realized the development was going seriously cattywampus and then they couldn't get rid of them fast enough. However, they didn't want to sell at a loss. So the odd if beguiling lots, initially appealing to those valuing rustic seclusion, sweeping vistas and (initial) affordability, had substantial deal-breakers built into them.

The consequence? For decades, the market was flooded with all-but-unsellable parcels.

Despite being offered dirt-cheap compared to similar regional properties, they found few takers once their bizarre pedigree — a seemingly jinxed development that had flown off the rails, rife with an angry-native social climate and a rejection by the larger community, bereft of infrastructure and burdened with a prohibitive cost to gain code compliance — became common knowledge to anyone doing the least bit of research.

But at the Vista's inception, such major stumbling blocks weren't evident beyond the apparent lack of infrastructure. With the Back-to-the-Land movement shifting into high gear, the tiny minority of older, relatively well-heeled parcel buyers, energized by the prospect of retiring together in their own little realm of secluded unspoiled nature, had seen in the far-flung, primitive development the chance to create their own cozy paradise. One to shape, mold and control as they saw fit.

And they hadn't been alone in their feel-good enthusiasm and optimism over the place's bright prospects.

Excited to have discovered such an affordable wonderland to vacation at, maybe someday retire to — at least a sure-fire investment — everyone and their uncle was jumping down the rabbit hole.

CHAPTER 8

Mt. Shasta Vista was, well... *different*

In some ways, the Vista, with its 1,641 two- to three-acre parcels, was a breed apart from other regional subdivisions emerging about the same time. And new rural subdivisions were popping up all over the region.

They included:

- Lake Shastina, just down the hill, with 3,200 lots averaging .2 to .3 acres each (one-tenth the size of Vista lots), started in 1968;

- Shasta Forest, in the McCloud area, with 791 lots of two-and-a-half to five acres each, launched in 1966;

- Juniper Valley (practically next door), with some 240 lots of varied 10, 20, and 40 acres each (four to 16 times larger than Vista's), exact founding date unknown;

- Klamath River Country Estates (KRCE), in the Hornbrook region, with 2,050 lots of one to 2.6 acres each, began in 1967; and

- Hammond Ranch, between Mt. Shasta and Weed, its association formed in 1969, with about 430 lots of .35 to .55 acres each

One big difference, apart from the obvious iffy water situation, was that Mt. Shasta Vista happened to be the first.

Just a seasonal camp

Started a year or more ahead of the rest, there was an as-yet-unproven market for rural developments, especially one of such sprawling scale. Developer Collins may have felt that the lots needed to be priced so low as to prove irresistible, attracting eager buyers and getting the ball rolling. As the region's first such developer, he may have considered it too risky to pursue a planned community that would require a vast infrastructure investment. Instead, he'd spring only for simple road access, signage and an informal community well and water truck. The place might be deemed too far from town to attract people wanting to live here, and so prove successful only as a seasonal, collectively owned, primitive vacation camp.

He played it safe, feeling no call to hammer together any master plan. He'd contented himself with launching a simple, bare-bones, de facto recreational development, as state law still allowed, one that might or might not become something more. He'd see what happened.

In a way, he was a little like a scientist running a test experiment. But an unobjective one, displaying a vague, tomorrow-never-knows air about its endless potential that undoubtedly influenced the experiment's test results.

Hedging bets

Even though he was surely aware of the Back-to-the-Land movement rapidly emerging at the time, shrewdly sensing a new rural land market, he also knew that potential buyers might resist the notion of building homes if they had to drill deep wells *and* extend power lines themselves.

Moreover, he must've known how up in arms the farming and ranching locals were over his invasive cockamamie scheme, so much so that he'd perhaps opted to go slowly in part to give them time to come to terms and accept the place, initially marketing the lots for seasonal camping. *Just visiting, folks, no worries.* He'd let the buyers deal with the angry hornet's nest of locals if they ever got brave enough to actually try moving onto the latter's now-lost wilderness.

In any event, the wording of the Vista's ruling documents (CC&Rs, or Covenants, Conditions & Restrictions) was your basic boilerplate legalese. Once the place's first few parcel holders dropped anchor and began rendering the original legal framework inadequate, this in itself might've spelled certain disaster without extensive revisions. Such a reworking was possibly deemed critical by at least some of the settlers — the more social, growth-minded, not the just-leave-us-alone faction — if the place was to have a solid avenue for building out with some rhyme and reason and guardrails to steer development in an agreed-upon direction.

The board lacked the power to fine

It might have created, for instance, the legal power for the board to fine errant owners for infractions of decided appearance parameters and home restrictions, like bans on changing vehicle oil, hanging out laundry and solid fencing, as some others would do, thus (ideally) working to maintain a particular agreed-on lifestyle of sorts. This power enabled the imposition of a lien on an owner's legal title if one chronically failed to pay for a ticketed infraction, thereby establishing at least a grudging respect for the rule of law. It would've served to discourage non-compliant behavior by property owners and possibly land hunters bent on inappropriate property use.

Of course, this was always a two-edged sword. As pointed out in the periodical *The Week*, quoting reporter Sarah Holder:

"About 74 million people in the U.S. live in community associations, mostly HOAs, *[homeowner associations]* which create their own regulations meant to keep behavior polite, aesthetics consistent, and property values high." But, she went on to say, "… the rules can be capricious and penalties for violations steep … One Colorado couple, Jose and Lupita Mendoza, say that a series of minor violations, like failing to remove a dead tree, snowballed into the HOA's foreclosing on their home despite their never missing a mortgage payment."

Without an overarching plan for residential growth or a vision beyond the general legal boilerplate, Mt. Shasta Vista was forever left to struggle, swimming upstream against the current. It was always vulnerable to the vagaries of the place's latest resident-owners' sometimes arbitrary dictates… even as the more socially minded among the fitful, ever-changing flock of dwellers hoped to transform the place from its primitive beginnings into an actual by-gosh, functional community. One that its dwellers might've actually taken pride in rather than only used and tolerated for a while.

Interest flatlines

With so many parcel owners absentee and seldom, if ever, visiting, from the start it seemed the overwhelming number of title holders were indeed only betting on the place and the anticipated actions of others: initially, that small minority of owners who enjoyed vacationing here, and later, the even smaller number who actually built houses and dropped anchor. Both were naturally inclined to work together to advance the place and improve its livability (and market value).

Surely they were the vanguard of others who would follow over time. Meanwhile, the investors and speculators were content to let actual residents do the heavy lifting. Maybe they liked to imagine them as an army of worker ants industriously building up the place and its value before they began enjoying it themselves. Or, far more likely, they cashed in and made a respectable chunk of change for their trouble.

As it turned out, it would prove to be more trouble than they could've imagined in their wildest dreams. Holders were destined to lose heart in droves not long after the development's early burst of improvement efforts faded and small-minded vibes swept the land, taking deep root.

The birth of a community well

Water was always a critical concern. By the early 1970s, visiting repeat campers and residents rallied, partnering with developer Collins to develop what soon became an informal community well with an impressive flow rate, just off Vista land on Juniper Drive. It featured a large holding tank with an overhead valve for rapidly filling 2,000-gallon water trucks and included a garden spigot, thereby serving both campers and well-less home builders. Collins, with his usual largess, sold the association a water truck for a dollar. About the same time, many contributed to the volunteer fund to extend electric power lines to the lots of any owners who committed to building to code. A long mobile home was pulled in near the front of Juniper Drive to hold the first few of the state-mandated monthly property owners' board meetings.

After this initial flurry of action, though, enthusiasm for group improvement efforts seemed to run out of steam. New and soon-to-be residents switched gears, scrambling to carve out their own little backwoods mini-kingdoms in the semi-wilderness. It was often all they could do to build up resources to provide for their own needs to some semblance of their long-accustomed standard of living.

As earlycomers constructed the place's first approved dwellings, it seemed to be shifting from a simple, de facto shared camp to the beginnings of a formal rustic community. Albeit one spread so thin amid the vast acreage that dwellings might've appeared surreally misplaced to any impressionable visitors who chanced to cruise the labyrinth of back roads: nothing but trees and brush for long stretches, until rounding a bend, then *bam!* a full-on estate jumped out at them.

Neither fish nor fowl

Interest in enjoying one's camping parcel must have nosedived overnight. Those who had roughed it camping were now themselves noisily building homes, or grumbling about those who were and intending to sell the first chance they got. To the recreationally minded, the place had lost its charm. The once collective-camping wilds were being cluttered with all the man-made trappings of civilization they'd come here to get away from. It was an oil-and-water situation, refusing to mix.

The place was now neither fish nor fowl. It was in an ungainly situation that provoked growing frustration among both dwellers and absentee owners.

Once unapproved shelters began to multiply, the realm's fledgling legal community, which residents had poured their personal fortunes into, representing lifetimes of blood, sweat, and tears, was in dire straits. Without updating the CC&Rs — or every future would-be resident dutifully toeing the line and meeting county health and building codes — residents faced an insurmountable impasse. They would be stymied at every turn, their most dedicated efforts to restore the place's brief upscale-rustic cachet as a respectable, admired fledgling community rendered futile.

Cruising block captains

Early on the association's few residents met to appoint informal block captains for each of the nearly seven square miles of land (two of its eight sections, 7 and 24, are only partial sections). They worked to alert other residents and lot owners to any suspicious activity within their respective domains, driving around regularly, scoping the scene and relaying the latest skinny to board members for review at the monthly meetings and addressing if deemed warranted.

This phase of organized grassroots government at least demonstrated a strong cohesion among many, if not all, of the early residents. (Cynics might read this as being motivated to protect their investment values more than anything.) Their rudimentary grassroots vigilance effort grew into an informal phone-tree hotline once too many barbarians began storming the gates to keep a handle on things at monthly meetings alone.

Civic-minded spirit

Even if their incentive was only to nip incipient health and building code violations in the bud, it at least demonstrated civic-mindedness, albeit more intolerant and exclusive than altruistic. One that might've served the place well in the long run, had it evolved from its initial reactive, law-and-order policing into a fair-minded, can-do, live-and-let-live mindset, willing to make the best of the situation. However, that wasn't going to happen. It was their way or the highway.

Some of the original older residents had by this time already moved on, devastated, their fondest dreams of enjoying retirement years in a sweet spot of peace and tranquility shattered. They didn't have the heart or, for some, the fortitude, to take arms against a sea of trouble and endure the ongoing battles with unruly interlopers invading their realm by mounting a desperate Hail Mary campaign to try restoring law and order.

Those who stayed, though, never say die, were ready to do battle. They demanded, with a barely-contained wrath off the Richter scale, that the county enforce its own friggin' codes, dammit.

But as more and more lot buyers boldly occupied the parcels they'd grabbed and seemingly defied anyone to do anything about it, it eventually overwhelmed weary county enforcement officials. It appeared they'd been outmaneuvered: They couldn't stem the tide of scofflaws with their limited workforce despite their most diligent efforts.

At some point, county officials threw in the towel and gave up on the place as a lost cause.

Result: The soon-to-be-minority, flying-by-the-seat-of-their-pants, shocked-senseless, respectable legal-residency that had elected to stay and who were now being routed in their code-enforcement battles with the unruly rabble, found themselves between the devil and the deep blue sea.

White elephant time forgot

Not surprisingly, with such a daunting series of snafus and the resulting chaos growing like weeds, public interest in the wayward development flatlined for decades. After it outgrew its first-generation, recreational-only use and then stalled in its attempt to be something more by accepted standards, its parcels were massively devalued in the marketplace.

The sprawling development became an unmanageable white elephant of odd lots, more trouble than they were worth trying to move and earn a paltry commission on, in the view of many regional realtors.

Perhaps it was not unlike other failed or semi-failed rural subdivisions that various ambitious California developers had launched over the years, such as the controversial 15,287 one-acre lots of California Pines, outside Alturas, in the northeast corner of the state. Or California City, "America's Largest Abandoned City," some *50,000* lots, spread over *204 square miles*, all platted and roads made, in the barren, treeless Mojave Desert.

Interestingly, California City was launched within a month of Shasta Vista, and both were by real estate developers from the L.A. area, with its wild realty-hustling history. Perhaps influences were at work — both terrestrial and celestial — that made it a time of unrealistic development visions. Like it and others, the residency-challenged, one-time de facto rec-land of Mt. Shasta Vista seemed destined to become yet another place time would forget. Or try to.

Determined to tune out local politics

Eventually, this suited more than a few Vista residents just fine, those who decided to stay despite all, or had bought homes from those who had bailed. And especially those who grabbed parcels and threw together modest shelters on the fly. Various dwellers, doing their best to tune out the long-simmering gnarly politics, grew accustomed to the rich solitude. The sometimes prevailing tranquility more than compensated for the place's many shortcomings. They relished the park-like setting that had inspired its initial incarnation as a happy-go-lucky co-op campground. So few residents amid so much undeveloped high-desert woodlands proved delightful.

But it was terrible for the myriad investors and speculators. They found it next to impossible to sell holdings that no longer held appeal beyond their low price, unspoiled seclusion and sweeping vistas. Such parcels, no longer dedicated to camping yet requiring substantial outlays to live on them legally, found few interested who were even remotely convention-minded.

And, again, it didn't help sales efforts that the place, from its conception, had gotten such a bad rap and been resented by longtime locals for having closed off and taken over their age-old backwoods stomping grounds. Or that it was seen as perpetually problematic by county authorities. Many of the latter no doubt played soothsayer at its start: "It'll be a disaster, mark my words; wait and see. Want to bet? I'll give you two-to-one odds."

The county had rejected the misbegotten infant left squalling on its doorstep, quickly consigning it to an indifferent bureaucratic orphanage, as it were. The more-aware land shopper sensed the place's bleak and contentious history, alert to the not-always-subtle negative vibes that often saturated the land.

The omnipresent signs shouting "No This," "No That," and "No The Other Thing" offered subtle clues there was trouble in paradise.

CHAPTER 9

'Just a matter of time'

Many parcel owners held onto their lots in the apparent boondoggle, even so: in a dime, in a dollar. They doubled down year after year, paying the piper in the guise of the annual assessment through gritted teeth, determined not to take a bath on what had at first seemed a sure thing. In denial, they felt their investments would pay off *some*day, that the lots would eventually prove a nice place for *someone,* just not them. A place where one could build a home or a vacation cabin and enjoy the camaraderie of congenial, fellow part-time and full-time backwoods dwellers once the place finally got itself together.

After ages, at last convinced the place seemed doomed to remain permanently off-kilter, many finally bit the bullet. As fed-up and disappointed owners unloaded the clunkers en masse, resigned to breaking even or even taking a loss, cheap parcels flooded the market.

But there were often few takers. This, despite the late 1970s' $1,250 to $1,750 asking price and easy terms, roughly the same price as they'd paid when adjusted for inflation. Those who would buy them were often themselves only other disinterested professional investors, making small side bets on the place and parking a bit of extra cash a while, hoping the right suc — er, *buyer,* would come along. Or they'd be other uninformed casual investors, infected with the latest round of speculation fever, stoked at buying so much land for so little: "It was so cheap, I couldn't resist; and the mountain view is really something."

Age-old dream

But beyond such calculated dice rolling, impulsive moves and hopeful, "some day" thinking, there was always a sprinkling of land buyers psyched at the notion of — novel idea — actually *moving* onto the parcels. Some, like me, were still willing to build to code (albeit grudgingly) to fulfill the age-old dream of becoming country gentry flirting with respectability. To us, the lots were pure catnip. Some wanted to make like Thoreau, living simply on the land and letting the rest of the world go by. Some may have hoped to establish home businesses over time (despite the county imposing severe restrictions or bans on them), others to commute to work from home, the Vista becoming something of a rural bedroom community.

Entirely too many, at least to the thinking of the teeth-gnashing, ax-grinding remnant of code-legal residents, seemed only to be looking for cheap land for instant residency. People who wanted to avoid city rent with its steep first and last plus security, or have a hideout in the outlands, dodging child support or an outstanding arrest warrant or two.

Even if it meant roughing it — drastically downscaling one's living standard by hauling in a derelict mobile home or trailer, setting up a tent or fashioning a ramshackle structure from scrounged materials. And generating, at best, primitive cesspools as a non-ecological waste-disposal means. *And* have to haul in every drop of water. *Plus*, needing to fire up a generator or go without go-juice. For even if a power line teasingly skirted their property line, it couldn't be hooked up to a structure without first satisfying the blizzard of code requirements.

It definitely made for primitive living on primitive land. But the heady sense of freedom it provided for so little seemed worth it, at least for a while. They'd cross their fingers and hope the powers that be would let *them* be. But with the eighties' still-prevailing, heavy-handed mindset of the Vista's conforming residents and strict code enforcement yet holding sway, there was fat chance of that.

Round and round...

And so the mirage of a Mt. Shasta paradise, a dreamy backwoods realm, undervalued and under-exploited, kept mesmerizing all sorts for all sorts of reasons. As the land kept seducing detached speculators, hopeful investors and would-be residents alike, a distinct pattern in owner relations with the parcels emerged.

Sporadic cycles of short-lived buying enthusiasm were followed by maybe a curious camp visit or two, and then a chronic absence of any interest whatsoever; ephemeral fantasies fostered by the dreamy land had been played out. This was commonly the lot owners' dance. Even after decades, hundreds of parcels still clung to their relatively pristine states, apart from the occasional campfire stone ring and driveway roughed in, perhaps a dead tree or two cut down, with slash pile left, a bit of brush cleared, an outhouse built if really ambitious, maybe a soon-abandoned trailer. But they kept attracting new impulsive buyers wowed by the land's trifecta of allure: generously sized, secluded wooded parcels; sweeping mountain views and dirt-cheap prices.

Powerless to resist such a bargain

Similarly, the long succession of casual small investors and speculators soon lost interest in the first beguiling lots and any belief in their profitability. Some parcels doubtless changed hands a half-dozen times or more over the years, always attracting new buyers powerless to resist the bargain properties. It was simply a place that, to all appearances, felt safely hidden from many of the more aggravating aspects of modern life.

The massive mountain's regal presence — it was *right there* — kept emanating its captivating, almost palpable force and attracting new buyers. Those leaning toward new age thinking felt it could overstimulate a person's upper chakras if their energies weren't grounded. On arrival, the thinking went, such people had imaginations and visualization powers overamped; the mind reeled, bursting with excited fantasies and visions of what all they'd do with the fabulous off-the-beaten-track properties they'd been lucky enough to snag.

In a way, it was California Dreamin' full tilt.

And so the luckless development kept spinning round and round on its own little short-boom, long-bust merry-go-round. Riders reached out for the elusive brass ring of easy country living or fast-turnover profit, while realtors, trying to make their nut by moving low-end "road kill" properties, supplied the band organ's shrill yet hypnotic melody.

Stymied by a sea of disinterested speculators and investors feeling nickel-and-dimed

It probably can't be overstated: Competing with the place's host of other drawbacks — water scarcity, lack of power, absence of development plans, often rocky soil and steep-sloping lots, incensed locals, a largely ineffective board and the prohibitive cost of meeting code — was, though subtle, in a way one of the most significant stumbling blocks of all: the adverse effect that the teaming sea of detached absentee lot owners had on the place. They'd sunk money into it and soon got disheartened, some bitter. So much so, they became indifferent to the needs of the subdivision if it were to ever save itself from itself, or came to think such a thing was impossible. Not if it meant forking over one more cent beyond what they were already forced to pony up each year. Such powerful collective discontent reinforced and locked in the profound sense of futility that infused the terminally wayward (albeit still charming) development.

They were chagrined to realize they'd gotten stuck with a soft-market lemon that, adding insult to injury, required the annual shelling out through the owner-association assessment; it left them feeling nickel-and-dimed to death. They felt they were paying for the upkeep of roads they themselves never drove on just so a few other lot owners could live here. Meanwhile, lot values stagnated. Such a feeling of acute buyers' remorse undermined even the most determined efforts of civic-minded residents to salvage the foundering place's onetime seeming promise and set it on more solid footing.

Aside from all the other problems, how could Vista ever move forward when 90% of the absentee owners harbored such indifference and apathy toward the notion of trying to redeem the place? Not if it meant sinking any more money into it through special assessments to fund project proposals. Not even if a project, like creating a modest community center, might increase parcel values, making the place more livable and thus parcels more desirable and easier to sell. That's how jaundiced and cynical absentee lot holders came to feel towards the luckless place.

To them, the place was a money pit, pure and simple.

Countless lot owners lost whatever faith they might've once held in the Vista and its potential to be anything other than the chaotic, infrastructure-shy disaster area that many of its few residents seemed to perversely prefer, for it left such an embarrassment of undeveloped, park-like land around them that the thoughtful, stuck investors had so generously provided.

Not another red cent...

Those who opted to keep the parcels despite everything, or tried to unload them but couldn't at a reasonable price, along with the latest round of new, soon-disillusioned owners, all felt they were burdened with, putting it bluntly, lame-ass properties in an ass-backwards development.

For what little it mattered, the annual membership assessment was far less than other regional rural subdivisions' (with the possible exception of next door's Juniper Valley). When I arrived in the late 1970s, the annual cost was about $20. (By 2025, it had grown to $300; while definitely having become ouchy, it was still easily one of the cheapest — nearby Lake Shastina's annual hit was some $2,200.) But no matter. They still felt shaken down for the latest assessment every September. Many no doubt felt like trailer-park mobile-home owners: The structure was theirs, but they had to pony up rent every month on the space it perched on lest it be seized in foreclosure… in the Vista's case, by the Mt. Shasta Vista Property Owners Association. Ironically, since every lot owner was a member, in some weird way it was like foreclosing on oneself.

Cynics thought the whole setup smacked of being a racket.

'Left for dead'

Perhaps predictably, due to the many absentee parcel holders' unmistakable disenchantment with the stuck-in-the-mud place — "left for dead" in another of the realty world's dark-humor insider phrases — the association often suffered late annual payments and nonpayments. Initial optimism for the place had long since evaporated, and as a growing share of absentee owners became reluctant to fork over every year, the wording on the annual billing statement got a mite testy. Key words in large black boldface letters defied ignoring the association's demand for prompt payment. They practically shouted:

PAY WITHIN 30 DAYS TO AVOID SEVERE PENALTY OR FORECLOSURE

Things were obviously a far cry from the lighthearted communication of earlier times with its merry spiels of carefree vacationing and cheerful visions of retiring to the enchanted land bye 'n' bye. Current circumstances had taken a dreary, hard, no-nonsense turn. The reason: Board members were grappling with how to keep enough revenue coming in to cover the constant maintenance needs of the 66 miles of cinder roads. Roads that would otherwise return to nature — and then have angry visiting owners hounding them to get on the ball or they'd refuse to pay. They were in a pickle, a Catch-22, a damned if they did and damned if they didn't situation, stuck between a rock and a hard place…

But such chilly exhortations only seemed to encourage some to finally blow off paying altogether. *They're daring me not to pay, huh? Well, hell, I think I'll take them up on that; they can have that damn parcel back… worthless piece of crap; why I ever bought into the screwy lotus land it I'll never know… 'FUBAR Acres' would be a better name for the friggin' place… mumble grumble…*

Sometimes iffy roads

As more people moved in, legally or otherwise, and the endless, fragile cinder roads took on increased wear and tear, the one-person road crew was often unable to service them all. And perhaps none anywhere up to the immaculate zen standards of earlier, simpler times. A time when there were far fewer residents and less than a hundredth the traffic. A time when the back roads seemed to encourage one to drive at a mosey and unwind from the highway and drink in the pleasant scenery that the hundreds of empty, unspoiled wooded lots provided. But the roads were fragile: One good gully-washer of a rainstorm could wash away the loose cinder topping and cut hazardous deep mini canyons into the sand beneath it on downhill stretches, even if it had just been groomed to perfection the day before.

A further crimp in the idyll of Vista living: The roads proved irresistible to mischievous kids, both locals and visiting grandchildren of over-indulgent residents of the playground-less place. They gouged donuts in the deep, freshly deposited cinders while roaring on their two-stroke chainsaws-on-wheels known as dirt bikes, creating abrupt, jarring driving dips for vehicles and remedial work for the already overtaxed road worker.

Again, this led more owners — especially residents — to protest paying for roads that weren't being kept up — at least not theirs — the lion's share going to the most heavily trafficked. Like, far and away, the most problematic of all: the long, steep uphill stretch of Perla Road at the front of Section 13, off Sheep Rock. It costs several thousand dollars a year to maintain, especially with so many residents and visitors ignoring efforts to make it a downhill-only road, marked by a wrong-way sign at its base. Constant steep uphill driving — usually to avoid extra miles to reach one's place — keeps tearing it apart, wheels scrambling for traction and gouging deep ruts.

Before 2015, some sparsely settled or unsettled regions might've never seen a road truck in a decade or more. And then, finally, often only after some visiting owner, driving hundreds of miles to vacation on their remote parcel, only to get stuck in deep sand on the home stretch and forced to call a tow truck, raised a royal ruckus. Rightly furious, they held the association board's feet to the fire, demanding reimbursement for the tow bill. Such ire would finally stir harried board members to scramble to address the neglected stretches of its more remote hinterlands — and raise the annual assessment fee to cover the increased workload, along with rising material costs, wages, insurance, workers' comp, gas…

Problems like these seldom made for happy campers.

This, in dramatic contrast to the first visiting owners. Those who so relished the sojourns to their parcels from 10 hours away that they eventually moved on to them. They dropped anchor with the infectiously high spirits prevailing in the late sixties through early seventies, when, as Buffy Sainte-Marie would sing, "God is alive, magic is afoot." A time when waves of feel-good euphoria might wash over one out of the blue, even if your drug of choice was only Valium or a good stiff martini.

CHAPTER 10

Land left undisturbed for generations

At its start, many Vista lots felt almost pristine (some still do). Sure, there were a few old rotting stumps from lumber baron Abner Weed's having scythed the area's tall timber early in the 1900s. The bulldozing required to build the road network scarred the fronts of some parcels. (The KRCE development northeast of Yreka was born similarly, re-purposing tree-harvested lands into rec lots and possible future home sites for nature-hungry city refugees.) Most Vista parcels were left undisturbed for generations after the tree harvest and the later creation of roads, and they rebounded as part of a rich, fragile high-desert woodland ecosystem. One that could enchant anybody able to appreciate its subtle, almost primeval lure. One who didn't need towering trees and crystal streams before respecting and resonating with nature.

The land held inviting groves of junipers. Some of the older or withered ones had magical, almost Day-Glo chartreuse moss growing on their northern sides. Velvety lichens grew atop deep-shaded, half-buried boulders. There were riots of delicate, colorful wildflowers in rich purple, lavender, yellow and red in spring and early summer. And the occasional stands or single tall pine trees. And dramatic rock outcroppings, sometimes perched on by a hungry mountain lion on the lookout for deer meandering through.

Many areas lent a protective atmosphere that invited one to wax poetic over. It struck more than a few as an enchanted realm where time seemed to stand still.

Ephemeral paradise

Fresh high-desert air, balmy sunshine, often-profound quietude, plus a giddy sense of freedom for being in such a secluded backcountry reigned over by the regal mountain… all had combined to inspire repeat vacation visits from over 600 miles away, trekking from the bottom of the long state to the top. Enough so to move the select handful to chuck city living and retire here to enjoy the blessings of secluded woodland living year-round. And so it was that the place briefly became a residential Eden for every nature-loving retiree making the urban exodus — and who had the bucks to build according to their accustomed living standard, which, happily, more or less coincided with the county's then rigorously enforced building codes.

But rumor had it that the very earliest comers — among them builders of a simple cabin structure on White Drive and another builder, far more ambitious, of the Spencer house on Heinzelman Drive — hadn't even needed building permits to construct their respective cabin and multi-story residence. Code enforcement had apparently yet to gain a solid foothold in the more remote hinterlands. If true, this may have set the precedent for subsequent owner-builders who felt they needed no more than their own permission to build whatever they wanted on their lots. And the building department was forever left playing catch-up, saying in effect, "Hey, you need a permit now… we mean it. Seriously…"

No more sketchy subdivisions

By the early seventies, California legislators had become so leery of unregulated developments like Mt. Shasta Vista that they passed a flurry of landmark regulations known as the Subdivision Map Act to henceforth cover any new subdivisions. "… [A] new attitude of comprehensive planning and environmental protection emerged," wrote realty attorney James Longtin. The Vista, along with other rural subdivisions in the region, had barely slipped in under the wire before regulatory changes made it impossible to spin out such bare-bones, quick-buck, often problematic rural developments any longer.

After it passed in 1974, developers were required to first obtain local approval and make legally binding commitments to provide all basic infrastructure for any new residential subdivision proposed. If approved, they or the legal management arm would be required over time to pay for public improvements such as parks, playgrounds, and community centers. It seemed that our place, though grandfathered in, came to feel intense pressure from the county — in turn feeling the heat for being under the gun of the state with its demanding new standards — whenever an owner wanted to build on their parcel in the primitive development so unabashedly bereft of the now-mandatory infrastructure requirements.

Would-be Vistan homesteaders who believed in dutifully following the rules found themselves jumping through all kinds of complicated, time-consuming and expensive hoops to gain the right to reside on their lots — the first and perhaps most daunting, before anything else once passing a perc test, being to bring in an approved well… often a fairly deep one… sometimes a really deep one… and hitting water… hopefully good water. And then install a septic system and shell out another substantial chunk of change to have electrical lines extended.

All before one could apply for a building permit.

Who'd want to live in the middle of nowhere?
To create or not create community

Maybe county officials had crossed their fingers, hoping there'd never be any who for some strange reason wanted to live on such raw, bone-dry lots out in the middle of nowhere. For each new building permit okayed would mean several long drives out to inspect and sign off on the numerous construction phases. They had better things to do.

Jumping ahead, disillusioned residents had better things to do than foster the dubious notion of building community. Polarized energies, bearing remarkably cynical attitudes and short fuses, discouraged it at every turn. More and more, people moved here to do their own thing and be left alone: hermits united. (Or disunited, in this case.)

It often seemed residents would work together for the common good reluctantly at best. A visit to a monthly board meeting, where the place's buzzsaw, contentious, dysfunctional attitude (or its flip side, the apathetic, what's-the-use? mindset) was on full display, offered a quick cure for anyone nurturing a misguided notion of trying to help out the misbegotten place.

Any vision beyond the usual volunteer fire department and rummage sales to support it — maybe, if ambitious, working to secure a grant to make the area safer from wildfires — didn't seem to fit in with the dirt-cheap lots and their unmistakable lack of infrastructure. One, of course, paid dearly for such amenities in your more developed subdivisions — paved roads, electricity, water, gas, sewage, fire department, security force. When you bought land at a steal, expectations were low to nonexistent. Some people, craving natural solitude more than anything, bought here expressly because it *lacked* such trappings. To their way of thinking, any hum of a structured rural community, residents scrambling to get on the same page, too often resulted in everyone getting in everyone else's business and cannibalizing each other's energy, resulting in the age-old, elusive dream of tranquil rustic living remaining but a wistful imagining.

Bewitched by the realm's charms

Not so for that first-wave of affluent modern-day pioneers of yore. They were so bewitched by the realm's charms during simpler, if more rigid and constrictive, times that they had invested their sweat, fortunes and fondest hopes into making the Vista their new home, sweet home.

Though ostensibly open to others joining them if they met code, they'd essentially given birth to a semi-exclusive enclave of urbane respectability, an embryonic hideaway sanctuary of decent folk determined to enjoy living far from the madding crowd. It would be a haven where they might enjoy their retirement years living amid the deep quietude of nature… while, of course, working to keep the riffraff out, which they felt was their legal right, even their moral duty. As a song lyric of the time went, they were "… going where the living is easy, and the people are kind."

Kind of something, anyhow, as it turned out.

'Welcome all' Vs. 'Up the drawbridge!'

Many among the second wave of new residents (actually more of a steady trickle), like those of the first wave, were grateful to be here. They were swept up in the grand pioneering adventure of it all: living in the recently opened scenic land, so few others around after having long endured teaming city and suburban life, glad to share their good fortune with whoever might arrive to help further populate the mostly empty place. They offered cheerful assistance, wanting to see the fledgling backwoods community flourish. To them, each new denizen of the sparse backwoods settlement was welcome as rain in a drought during the heady late-frontier days of the 1970s.

These more outgoing, live-and-let-live neighbors were usually residents of dwellings whose original inhabitants had fled once Vista living began to lose its luster and what they'd once deemed a rare gem seemed to be suspiciously morphing into cheap paste. The second-generation newcomers hadn't experienced the latter's challenges in complying with exacting codes only to have others blatantly ignore them, eroding the place's short-lived cachet as an idyllic retirement enclave. And they didn't bear battle scars from the earlier rampant vandalism and theft by mischievous and malicious local offspring during the earliest, visiting-only years.

They were more upbeat, happy-go-lucky, eager to share their good fortune and excitement for being here. Some would invite newcomers like me to share an afternoon "drinky-poo" on their front porch, and offer to freeze water in repurposed milk jugs to help one weather 100-degree F. heatwaves — even generously invite this unprepared newcomer to winter in a vacant cabin.

Not their kind

Others, almost invariably among the first wave, weren't nearly so hospitable. Too many newcomers were *clearly* not their kind. Since there were no guardrails in place, no finely tuned CC&Rs to guide the place, each new arrival was instead summarily vetted. Bearing a no-nonsense stance, they'd quickly deem each newcomer either one who would conform to the code and tenuously fit in, reinforcing the nascent respectable community, or one who would stick out like a sore thumb and undermine the place's new order of things. They felt the latter needed to be dealt with in a gloves-off manner with all due haste, surgically excised from the realm like a dread malignant tumor.

Whereas they had done the heavy lifting and fought battles of attrition against the sometimes-hostile local population, conforming newcomers felt free to relax and enjoy the fruits of the former's labor. They savored the moment and embraced the place's tranquility. They relished the deep seclusion and appreciated those around them, regardless of a newcomer's circumstances or intentions.

Even though many firstcomers ground their teeth and poisoned their minds over how nonconforming undesirables were trespassing in their magical hideaway, such bad energies were blunted by the afterglow of the exultant pioneering spirit vibe still lingering in the air. It was a vibe that the more mindful felt, a sense of wonder and gratitude for having carved out places to live in Mt. Shasta's backwoods. Anyone who valued quiet living amid nature — or what at first appeared to be quiet living — treasured and relaxed into it.

But if the place were going through one of its periodic flare-ups, meltdowns or calamities, then they'd have to try weathering the storm. Sometimes they succeeded, other times, if some terrible incident like an isolated shooting occurred, (usually domestic incidents), they bailed.

Instant homestead, furious neighbors

More's the pity, but the first and remaining residents were no longer blissfully unwinding in well-earned retirements. Their long-anticipated golden years were being contaminated with baser metals. They got bent into pretzels under the endless trials they had to endure just when they thought they could finally relax. Unlike their former fellow founding neighbors, who, disillusioned and alarmed, sold out on the wings of the rapidly unraveling scene, they were made of tougher stuff. They dug in hard. Here for the duration, come hell or high water, any peace of mind they might have briefly savored vanished in the ongoing struggle to try to regain sovereignty over the realm they'd forged.

They scrambled to pull up the drawbridge and throw away the welcome mat, even as the entrance signs, in supreme irony, kept welcoming one and all. But, more in keeping with residents' less-than-friendly attitude, the big signs just beyond the now-hollow greeting snarled at drivers, as if daring them to enter and promising dire consequences if they did so without good reason. They reflected the trials and tribulations the first-comers had endured, facing a torrent of challenges: the hostility of the larger community resenting the place's very existence; over 1,000 absent lot holders, many seemingly jealous, mad or indifferent to the place's fate; the constant intrusion by the idly curious and sometimes mischief-minded; and now instant homesteaders, thinking to declare themselves home without paying the price of admission.

The earliest residents had been bound and determined to try arresting this intolerable trend by flexing no-nonsense authoritarian muscle and kicking serious butt. They'd get the unruly rabble thrown out — and, by god, *keep* the buggers out. Talk of installing entrance gates was probably mulled over but rejected as too impractical and problematic (the same as the much-later growers, facing epidemics of thievery, busts and hold-ups, would consider and dismiss a half-century later).

Somehow, they *had* to save their rural outpost from getting overrun by the rabble, undesirables with the unmitigated gall to invade their would-be respectable rural enclave on the cheap. Especially those revved-up younger folks of threadbare means… most especially those pot-smoking hippies and beer-guzzling redneck bikers, plus the peculiar new hybrid, the pot-smoking, beer-guzzling redneck-hippie, all of whom they thought they'd forever left behind in the cities.

Girding their loins

They knew such instant settlers would be worlds away from ever deferring to their tight-wound, conventional ways and thus prove disastrous. That is, if they'd ever given them a leg to stand on, which they didn't. They mobilized to get them evicted post-haste, determined to nip the insufferable situation in the bud. Girding their loins, they took on a sea of trouble with a ruthless full-court determination: damn the torpedoes and full speed ahead. They *demanded* that every property holder earn the right to live on the land, just as they had, end of story. They *had* to meet all health and building code requirements, no matter the cost, time or effort. If you couldn't afford it, or didn't want to go down that path for some reason, well, tough; the place obviously isn't for you. So don't even think about it, bub.

But word of the cheap, secluded parcels spread. The floodgates of land-search postings opened wide once realtors started advertising lots for sale cheap by the dozen on their coast-to-coast multi-listing network. So, despite residents' best efforts to deter further would-be, unqualified newbies from invading the now-endangered paradise and insist that existing miscreants either conform or scram, it would prove a losing battle. But they never gave up; the home guard sailed clear around the bend, permanently unhinged. Nursing boundless rage as they tried throwing their weight around to enforce their zero-tolerance stance, in a way they became no different than the wider community who'd been so blindly intolerant of *them*.

While some among the pretenders to the realm, again, no doubt had the bucks to build an approved shelter, they instead opted to go outlaw in effect, not bothering to seek a county bureaucrat's blessing for what they did on their own remote property. Why sink a fortune building on such cheap land? It didn't compute. Others, of more modest means, were content to set up long-term tents, pull in a trailer or mobile home, or build a little tumbledown shanty from scrap material. Regardless of their situation, they hung their hats and figured they were home.

The firstcomers lumped them all together. It's not much of an exaggeration to say they dismissed them as little better than criminals. They were a viral infection threatening the health and well-being of the realm's legitimate tax-paying residents and must be eradicated at all costs.

CHAPTER 11

Brazen newcomers

I suspect that the brazen newcomers, in turn, must've been either oblivious or indifferent to the established residents. Why should they care what a few scattered, uptight retirees, many living miles away, thought of them or their presence amid the giant remote checkerboard of mostly empty lots? It must've been either "What's the big deal?" or "Mind your own business." Many likely weren't unduly concerned over the county ordinances they were openly defying, having tuned out the barking signs as mostly paper-tiger bluster and toothless desperation. It seemed that living on remote land could quickly dull the notion of conforming to what were considered unreasonable demands. It was the legal gobbledygook of city-living mindsets, born of the over-complicated realities of so many living so closely together. News flash: Mt. Shasta Vista wasn't a city.

The happy illusion of one's secluded Vista property being a stand-alone lot, existing independently of any outer control — rather than in fact one among 1,641 lots, each ostensibly subject to a sea of county, state and federal regulations — was too seductive not to succumb to. In fact, it might be said that one's sense of well-being and peace of mind fairly *depended* on it.

So it went that the intimidating 'No This,' 'No That,' and 'No The Other Thing' signs were dismissed as unenforceable bluff. Well-heeled residents were trying to bogart the place by demanding everyone conform to their la-di-dah living standards or else. But more and more, newcomers went their own way, "doing their own thing", that vital watch phrase from the Sixties being taken to heart by greater numbers with each passing year. Society was unwinding and jettisoning the former times' fading tense, authoritarian mindset of rigid conformity — again, the lingering vestige of the horrific World War II period that bent the world's collective mindset so grievously out of shape that it took decades to recover from it.

When errant newcomers were rudely awakened after an unpleasant confrontation or two with compliant residents who'd gone nuclear and summoned all-business county enforcers, it no doubt did little to make them want to comply even if they could afford to. The firstcomers, in their scramble to preserve the predominantly La La Land-ish, country club enclave from rack and ruin, had adopted such a furious stance against the newcomers who dared to ignore the codes that the more rebelliously-minded land buyers, scoping their overwound headspace, thought, *Well, screw 'em, uptight bastards; we'll take our chances.*

Fraught, distraught and overwrought

While the firstcomers had obediently conformed to every last residency requirement and expected each would-be resident to do the same, it seemed such rules soon became an endangered species. With a growing spirit of anarchy emerging amid fast-changing times, the place grew progressively dysfunctional, embroiled in escalating battles over lifestyle and code compliance.

The way its citizen deputies patrolled the roads, looking for wrongdoing wherever it might lurk, the place at times must've felt like it was practically under martial law. The sad truth was that their fledgling one-time safe-haven backwoods retirement enclave was turning into its own madding crowd; they were irretrievably losing it.

Not all newcomers were probably such brazen anarchists. Actually, maybe very few at first. Some must've been, by and large, no doubt law-abiding folks, only nurturing hopes of living out simpler versions of tranquil country living due to the lack of wherewithal to meet the county's daunting code-compliance demands. They probably couldn't believe that anybody would actually enforce the sign's growling warnings in such an isolated area. Or that people living miles away could get so rattled over how others were living on their own property, minding their own business.

So, while the code non-conformers might've had no real intent to buck the system per se, their fondest dreams of living the good life were blown to smithereens if receiving an antagonistic 'unwelcome wagon' visit from hitherto unknown neighbors from hell, an overbearing delegation of high-and-mighty hard-asses who swooped down on them out of nowhere and read them the riot act.

Others were thicker-skinned. More ungovernable and less concerned with rendering unto Caesar, they dug in hard and kicked back, giving as good as they got. In the early 1990s, an unsanctioned neighbor with such confrontational tendencies had just been given his walking papers from the board. One day he spotted the board president driving about. He began aggressively tailgating him for miles along the otherwise empty back roads, sticking to him like glue. While the man no doubt must've become alarmed on looking in his rear-view and seeing he'd gained the ire of some crazed, bearded madman, one might've concluded he was only reaping what he and earlier board members had sown for copping such an intolerant attitude.

Lookin' for a home back of beyond

Flashing back again to the early to mid 1970s… After the first wave or two of settlers had arrived, following the few late sixties' early birds, a sprinkling of maybe 40 to 50 year-round, still mostly compliant residences dotted the landscape. While the code-defiant trend had yet to gain a serious foothold, the momentum, matching the dizzying speed of changing times, was doubtless building. For the genie was out of the bottle: There was cheap land near Mt. Shasta waiting to be snapped up and settled on by anyone not too concerned about some distant bureaucracy's notions of how they should live on it. Various and sundry leaped at the chance to make the Vista's sprawling juniper boonies their home, too.

In the bigger picture, the idea of one not just visiting but actually living in nature had taken off. "Head for the hills, brothers!" was the clarion call as city-weary souls from every walk of life joined the Back to Nature movement. For some, it would prove just a few years' respite from urban or suburban living; for others like me, it would become an enduring new lifestyle.

As nature-loving people's interest in making the great escape from the frustrations of city living soared, the Vista took on something of the air of a time-release Oklahoma Land Rush. In leaps and bounds, excited new arrivals discovered the affordable backwoods, staked their claim, and settled in. Or tried to. With the place having no master plan and the once-iron grip on code enforcement destined to gradually loosen, each newcomer went for it, winging it, flying blind, to develop their own little piece of terra firma.

The area experienced fitful, frenzied bursts of house construction, and as time passed, fewer and fewer were built to code. Sounds of hammering, whining circular saws and power generators filled the air. I'd guesstimate that by the mid to late seventies, maybe 70 to 80 residences of markedly varied degrees of ambition and code compliance were dotting the remote woodlands — a woodlands that, as became more evident over time, seemed to exist in its own special world.

Those opting to ignore code requirements and play it by ear in the frenetic scramble to settle were no doubt intent on getting a toehold while the getting was good. It was always harder to tell someone they couldn't be there after they'd fenced off the property, built a shelter, moved in, lock, stock and barrel, and posted their own signs, "Posted No Trespassing" and 'Private Property Keep Out' being popular.

The territorial imperative was indeed something to be reckoned with.

With so many hypnotized by the land in a way that might

preclude any more practical concerns, a strange wonderland was emerging, one growingly at variance with mundane reality despite the most dedicated and frenzied efforts of its outraged compliant residents to arrest the insufferable trend dead in its tracks.

Spirit of 'anything goes' gains traction

It's unknown whether some of the seriously invested firstcomer residents ever considered revising the CC&Rs. Conceivably, it might've enabled a more orderly growth into a standard community, one in which things were more specifically spelled out and one knew they'd have to toe the line and don winter wear to deal with the blizzard of health and building codes. This, for better or worse, was the accepted reality of places like nearby Lake Shastina, and, again, most any American city or suburb in the country.

But not in the Vista, exceptional problem child that it was. Though first settled by conventional law-abiding citizens, it was the rebellious Sixties and early Seventies. Many long-accepted ways were being seriously challenged; authority was being questioned. It was inevitable that the era's spirit of Anything Goes would soon burst their happy bubble, mindsets locked in the Nifty Fifties, like it didn't exist.

Perhaps the situation was aided and abetted by the early vacationers themselves. They'd built up such an exuberant (if law-abiding) spirit on the land, a freedom-mindedness that might've eclipsed concern for social sensitivity and mundane realities. That is, beyond conforming to code. Each was determined to be king or queen of their own regal wilderness mini-realm and doing whatever it took to preserve it and the surrounding land — even turning in a nonconforming neighbor. Still, one wonders whether such a CC&R revision might've helped the place gain a firmer foothold.

A moot point, though. With 98% of the property owners absent and living all over the country — many by then nursing serious buyer's remorse — they would've realized they'd never get the two-thirds vote needed to tackle such a costly and time-consuming legal restructuring. And, besides, they were retirees. Once building their new homes was a done deal, their days of heavy lifting were over beyond tackling such weighty issues as whether to paint the living room taupe or beige, or go with the 2-to-3 or 4-to-6 person capacity Jacuzzi.

Or so they'd hoped.

Bogarting Paradise

The more cynical view, again, might've held that the first year-round residents realized constructing full-on homes amid a sea of raw parcels once a camp land was bound to create certain thorny problems. But they didn't care. They had theirs for whatever remained of their time on earth; let the chips fall where they may. And, anyhow, since the lots were in fact zoned for single-family residency, the new dwellers must've thought, *Hey, what's the big deal? They're zoned for residences; camping was only a first-generation use of the parcels, right?*

But they surely would've realized that if enough lot holders *didn't* join their ranks, the overwhelming majority of raw parcels, ruined for camp retreats, would be left in limbo, languishing undeveloped, unattractive as building sites due to the extra construction costs and remoteness. They must've realized that the market for the seemingly now-unusable lots would all but disappear.

Maybe the more considerate yet pragmatic among them were more, "No question about it, it's a shame. But, hey, it was always buyer beware. Everybody realized that at one point, it became every lot owner for himself."

The way they saw it, they'd earned the right to claim the place for themselves, along with any other lot holders also willing to build up to snuff. They'd complied with every last golblamed, nit-picky, pricey, time-consuming, peace-of-mind-frying legal residency requirement the bureaucracy had seen fit to throw at them. And wasn't it the developer himself who first suggested retiring here "bye 'n' bye"? Blame *him* if the parcels no longer served as the backwoods retreats you bought them to be.

And blame him they would. But the residents, too, for taking over the place and sometimes being less than gracious and accommodating to visiting owners still hoping to eke out a pleasant camping experience on their properties — properties whose useful shelf life had apparently just expired. Instead, they might've been rubbernecked as residents drove by, not stopping to say howdy, or, at best, offer a rushed exchange and maybe a few pointed words like, "You know, you can only camp here 30 days, don't you?" Their curtness would burst the would-be happy campers' bubbles and leave them feeling almost like intruders on their own land.

'And if we *can't* get you out... '

In any event, perhaps not unreasonably, the legal, tax-paying homeowners reigning over the land expected prompt county code-enforcement response to keep their newborn rural community respectable. Later, while still loaded for bear even as the system began failing them, their resolve shifted to venomous retribution: *And if we* can't *get you out, then, by god, we'll do our damnedest to make your lives here a living hell.*

For better or worse, the shape-shifting, neither-this-nor-that place was left a blank canvas. One to be painted on and painted over, and painted over again to whatever the latest in an ever-changing succession of residents and visiting campers aspired the Vista to be (if anything). Each of the more dominant and involved inhabitants in a given period advanced their own notion of how things should be, trying to convince others that it was the best, or the only, way to go.

At the same time, the rest just wanted to be left alone to rusticate in peace. The situation was akin to excited kids building a sandcastle on the shore until the high tide rushes in and, in a twinkling, erases even the most ambitious efforts. Later, new castles are built by others, likewise unmindful of the next rising tide. Or like creating an image on the then-popular Etch-a-Sketch toy, and, with a shake of the hand, even the most elaborate design vanishes as if it never existed.

Dime a dozen

While legal requirements for homebuilding ostensibly fell within the sphere of county, state and federal authorities working together — which ordinances and codes the development's future parcel owners were then ostensibly obligated to conform to — these were never easy to enforce by the understaffed team tasked with such matters. A tiny dwelling amid a sprawling 66-mile labyrinth of private unpaved roads in the middle of nowhere was not easy to track. Or even be aware of as existing, short of poring over satellite photos, which, of course, in time became the county's standard procedure for boosting property taxes for lot improvements.

Once, my neighbor Steve found that his annual property tax assessment had gone up. He inquired and was told it was because he'd installed a new metal roof on his seasonal cabin, thereby constituting an improvement. He successfully argued that it wasn't an improvement, but only replacement maintenance for an existing structure. They lowered the assessment back.

Perhaps being a smidge over-helpful, the livid code-compliant residents burned up the phone lines, screaming bloody murder over the latest noncompliance they uncovered, expecting a rapid response as if the fate of the world depended on it — as, indeed, the fate of their own little private world did.

Tall order

But it was a tall order. In the fast-changing times, with the heady sense of freedom living in the secluded back-country enclave gave its new dwellers, compliant and "outlaw" alike — often no one else living within a quarter mile or more in a county too poor to hire enough workforce to enforce its own codes should enough choose to ignore them — something of a striking libertarian, even anarchistic, spirit took root. Especially among the system-defiant, minimalist-lifestyle baby boomers, who, fast on the wings of the earlier waves, felt pulled to the mountain like a tractor beam on TV's "Star Trek: The Next Generation."

They weren't about to be told how to live on their own property, especially by a bunch of uptight old-fogy fuddy-duddy busybodies.

Parcels, once losing their brief upscale-rustic cachet of respectability after being irreversibly compromised for retreat use, began flooding the market at a dime a dozen. Excited land-hunters might not have stopped to wonder *why* they were going so cheap. It may have struck them as simply one of the last few feel-good land deals around, and they'd been lucky enough to discover the gems before someone else. While it might've seemed an extraordinary deal, too good to be true, land-hungry buyers may have liked to believe that such pricing only reflected how things *should* be.

Affordable living; what a concept.

—— **CHAPTER 12** ——

Doing your own thing

Such a free-wheeling spirit might've been fine, had the place built a solid foundation of infrastructure support and appropriate CC&Rs. Obviously, it didn't. Cheap land really could create cheap intentions. The place's recreational-use period had run its course, and the tiny group of legal residents was now desperately trying to keep the place code-compliant. But the varied crowd of instant homesteaders was slowly but surely growing, psyched to do their own thing. Not one of them bought into the retirement community's notions of how things *should* be done.

During the radical late Sixties to early Seventies — as different generations, headspaces, lifestyles, incomes, awareness levels, land-use intents and varied respect for the rule of law threw themselves together in one glorious mess within the giant cookie-cutter of a bare-bones subdivision— it often seemed as though the only thing everyone agreed on was to disagree with everyone else.

The growing unwillingness of so many to build to code was of course driven by a refusal to appease the powers that be if it meant having to spend a fortune one didn't have before being able to create even a modest living shelter on one's own land. The ensuing rebellion against building codes, viewed as oppressive, tore to shreds what little of the place's threadbare social fabric and sense of community had been knitted. It sparked the long-pitched battles between the staunchly compliant who stayed, braced for battle, and the merrily (and not so merrily) rebellious who arrived and likewise dug in hard. During those astonishingly polarized times, the former viewed the latter as illegal land squatters, fully deserving the bum's rush, while the latter viewed the former as uptight control freaks with too much money and a serious need to chill.

Many elements made for a place so festering with irreconcilable differences that it sabotaged itself to death. A place built on such shaky footing, lacking water, electricity and fine-tuned CC&Rs; a *What code?'* attitude; an overwhelmed county's inability or unwillingness to enforce the codes effectively; contentious energies aimed at it by disgruntled locals, resenting their existence… all were baked into the monumentally unlucky development. Such a laundry list of hindrances all but guaranteed that whatever elusive hopes the more civic-minded residents and concerned property holders might've nurtured, hoping to turn the place around, were doomed six ways to Sunday.

The property owners' board, a.k.a. 'the gestapo': Hardball with a vengeance

Reflecting and amplifying the place's many woes was the Mt. Shasta Vista Property Owners Association (MSVPOA) board of directors. Formed to fulfill the ongoing legal obligations of a nonprofit public-benefit corporation, the board was composed of six elected volunteer landowners serving staggered two-year terms and met monthly. Any lot holder in good standing was eligible to run.

In the earliest years, it mainly focused on road maintenance and signage. For a while, it appointed a "sunshine committee" to send get-well cards to some in their aging circle who had perhaps waited too long to retire and enjoy their golden years. (The stresses of an unpleasant situation had likely aggravated their already fragile health.) Since, to be eligible, all board members had to live in approved structures and be in good standing (that is, having paid the annual dues), or at least be current if living elsewhere, the board naturally led the charge in declaring war on the scourge of non-compliance running amok.

Universal health and building code compliance in Vista had been critical, especially for a legal resident who planned to move on and hoped to get a good price for their place. Once they realized the good ship Vista was sinking fast by the port bow, their outrage was magnified for the bleak situation hitting the money nerve. They knew they'd lose any chance of a reasonable return after all their hard work and expense in creating standard residences, since the place had lost its brief pedigree as an enviable backwoods domain of respectable oldsters. Indeed, maybe it was this, more than being such strict law-and-order zealots per se, that triggered the lion's share of their wrath. Their friends, moving on, selling their places at a loss, wouldn't have wanted to if the place had remained compliant. They faced the same dire situation.

Such infuriated board members, in doggedly reporting every violation their minions' dedicated snooping uncovered, developed a stony policy of scorched-earth overreach and ruthless hardball tactics that was destined to become the downer gravity center of the realm for ages.

Serenity now!

Building a fence without a permit? Report the bugger. Thirty-two days camping out? Get that lawless interloper thrown off. In the course of such efforts, they alienated everyone who hadn't made a similar commitment to adhere to strict code specifications and their enforcement. Sometimes they upset even those who'd bought an approved home. They began to court serious misgivings for having moved into such a squirrelly place. Too late, they realized it was a hornet's nest, an outback zoo where it seemed it was normal for everyone not busy escaping the contentious air by getting drunk or stoned, or both, to be gnashing their teeth over one grievance or another.

An all too common lament: "What were we *thinking*, moving here?"

For decades the place experienced what many deemed no less than a mini-reign of terror. Various board members and their camp followers went about with such balls-out ruthlessness in confronting miscreants that it was scary. They tried their damnedest through every lawful means possible to stamp out the affliction plaguing the once-was-and-by-damn-and-by-Jesus-will-be-or-should-be-again, serene backwoods enclave of upright, God-fearing, law-abiding citizens… and everyone else could go to blazes.

Ah, the serenity of country living.

It came as no great surprise, then, that such dizzying intolerance made the place undesirable for many to ever consider moving into. Doubtless, it scared away some of your like-minded, would-be code-compliant owner-builders from settling on their lots. Prospective and new buyers heard the war stories from sullen or spitting-mad residents they approached to ask how they liked living here. And they likely got weary sighs and rolling eyes from health and building department workers the second they uttered the dread realm's name.

While time ultimately proved the code-conformity battle a lost cause, a whack-a-mole effort that did little to stem the tide of unsanctioned building and residency in the long run, it remained a cause kept simmering on the back burner; "The law's the law" remained the hardline stance, for all the good it did. The issue swept up everyone into the fray, or tried to; there were no innocent bystanders. Those who refused to take a side — "Sorry, we didn't move out here to get mixed up in any local politics" — were scornfully dismissed as do-nothing enablers and so part of the problem.

Man the battle stations

The enforcement system they'd depended on was failing them abominably: It had allowed barbarians to storm the gates… and *stay*. Shocked over their vision of peaceful retirement and living among kindred souls in the bosom of nature going to hell in a hand basket, some indeed seemed to take a certain grim, warped-out satisfaction in trying to exact a pound of flesh from every transgressor they encountered. For as long as they were still talking to them, they warned them of the dire consequences if they didn't toe the line, and they needed to believe it was true. Even when they knew such threats had become mostly empty bluster, they must've felt that in so freely venting their spleens, they'd make at least some feel so unwelcome that they'd start packing just to get away from such whack-job neighbors, hell-bent on trying to make their lives miserable.

Some of the more unwitting transgressors, having no stomach for testy confrontations and wars of attrition, indeed then gave up and moved on, feeling stunned and devastated. (I almost became one.) A few knew they were probably courting trouble, but weren't too attached to the lots so cheaply gotten, and so shrugged and left muttering, "Oh well, worth a try." But others, having thicker skins and more combative natures, dug in and escalated right along with the would-be enforcers, as if daring them to do their damnedest. They fenced off their places and posted their *own* gnarly signs. One of the more chilling: beneath a cross-hairs symbol, the stark warning,

If you can read this you're within range

Others, perhaps having too much time on their hands, actually seemed to enjoy taunting the sometimes bumbling, blustering enforcement crowd; it was an engaging cat-and-mouse game that in some weird way defined their stay and kept the adrenaline flowing.

There was yet another reason for the code-compliant to scramble to battle stations, Klaxon horns blaring to wake the dead: The volunteer board of directors of Mt. Shasta Vista, a nonprofit mutual-benefit common-interest corporation, was legally required to make a good-faith effort to ensure its association members complied with every applicable county, state, and federal law, statute and ordinance. Technically, the board could be held legally liable if found negligent in enforcing them; board members could be sued.

As if to show there could be no doubt whatsoever that they weren't shirking their duties, they reported every last infraction their diligent searches for wrongdoing unearthed.

But short of extralegal vigilante efforts, the place was entirely at the mercy of the county powers-that-be to keep things copacetic. Once the Vista started derailing, it was still up to the county to try to make things right. As taxpayers and association members, with the board having no legal fining powers, old-guard residents held that the stretched-thin county enforcement agencies were duty-bound to successfully resolve the intolerable situation and return the realm to 100% code compliance. No matter how long or how much effort it took, or how much it might cost.

For what earthly good were such ordinances if not enforced? Failing that increasingly impossible dream as the overwhelmed, underfunded enforcement system broke down, at least then it'd be on them. (And then maybe *they'd* get sued.)

Instantly radicalized

While each land buyer indeed signed an agreement to abide by all aforesaid laws, regulations and ordinances when buying a parcel, it was of course buried in a boilerplate sea of legalese fine print. So, beyond the more flagrant scofflaws of latter times were those who, in the rush to pursue elusive dreams of country living, were in blissful ignorance that they'd ever agreed to any such thing. They were shocked silly when told, often with a fire-breathing intensity, how you couldn't do this or that and don't even think about the other thing.

People came to feel foolish and misguided for having responded to the siren call of affordable land and what at first blush had seemed a relaxed, charming place (apart from those weird signs). The place seemed perversely bound and determined to give new meaning to the phrase 'going off the deep end', as if in some bizarro alternative universe and out to earn the Guinness World Record title for 'Most Dysfunctional Subdivision'.

The hardball tactics could radicalize one against the local powers that be in a heartbeat.

The more cash-strapped, instant-sanctuary sort of newcomers, hoping to buck the system, only knew they'd snagged an affordable piece of rural California; they were psyched to do their own thing and be left alone. Maybe over time they'd try for a well; maybe not. They'd connect with kindred souls who'd advise them, "Hey, just ignore the board; I do — hell, everyone does. It's just a toothless tiger, buncha retired power-freak busybodies with nothing better to do than try telling others how to live. Screw 'em and the horses they rode in on."

The very nature of any good-sized rural subdivision — a crazy-quilt gridwork of myriad lots tucked in the boonies — could make things problematic even *with* supporting infrastructure and CC&Rs. While it enabled anyone so inclined to buy a bit of rural land affordably — rather than, say, shell out for a far pricier stand-alone 10-, 20-, 40- or 80-acre parcel and then have to deal with road access and maintenance on one's lonesome — the hidden costs of affordable rural subdivision lots could prove steep indeed. People found themselves living amid a potluck assortment of strangers concentrated together in the middle of nowhere and mandated by law to cooperate, yet they were isolated far from the high-density town and city lifestyle that made such a plethora of rules and regulations feel normal… and so insufferable in the hinterlands.

It was that intense, super-regulated, soul-numbing urban reality that many had wanted to get away from that led them here in the first place.

Sharing the fantasy

The fact that people wanted their own land — a place where they could live in nature, a respectable distance from others — often made it difficult, given the contentious forces at play, to ever come to terms with the reality that others were sharing it. This, despite being a far thinner density than your typical urban scene. While you often couldn't see another's house from your own property, lending the illusion that you had a larger area to yourself than you actually did, everyone was, for better or worse, inextricably bound together on the mundane level in an overarching legal structure with endless edicts and restrictions. It felt as though the bureaucratic city mindset had been surre-ally superimposed on the untamed countryside. Thus, hopes that the place would offer carefree, independent country living were often cruelly dashed.

Steve Dockter was a longtime part-time neighbor, living a half mile away in what was likely the oldest structure in our section, built by two brothers from San Francisco. It had been unoccupied for decades and was going to rack and ruin when he bought it and brought it back to life. He led a gypsy existence, living on a sailboat in La Paz, Baja California, half the year and coming and going between here and the coast the rest of the time, working as an itinerant carpenter. His laconic, deliberate manner of speech and droll wit bore a striking resemblance to that of the actor Sam Elliot. One day, he noted wryly, "People need to learn to share the fantasy."

I knew what he meant. While many felt like they owned 20 or 40 acres because of a substantial buffer zone of vacant lots around their parcels, they needed to allow others to enjoy the same illusion by being mindful of their needs and rights. Otherwise, the potential for ceaseless territorial squabbling, indifference and thoughtless behavior could — and often did — result in a chaotic, wild-west social climate that could ruin it for everyone.

No surprise, the Vista's laundry list of neighborhood grievances often seemed endless.

Between barking dogs, roving packs of the same, discharging firearms, blasting stereos, gunning vehicle engines, driving fast and recklessly, vandalizing and stealing road signs, burning toxic materials in backyards rather than recycling or hauling waste to the dump, tree poaching epidemics, juvenile dirt bikers roaring about and tearing through the unfenced lots of absentee owners, epidemic roadside littering and mindless garbage dumping, strong winds blowing one's property detritus to the four corners with no concern over its despoiling the landscape… between all these things eroding blissful country living, there was usually always something or other to raise one's hackles.

'You see, it's complicated'

In sheer exasperation, residents kept up a constant stream of complaints to the mostly powerless Vista board, usually to no avail — and to county authorities. They, in turn, were often entangled in the slow bureaucratic process, with mindsets reflecting the conservative rural ways of an older populace, and often feeling helplessness, hostility or indifference towards the development that their predecessors had shown the poor judgment to approve.

Among those benumbed or burned out on elected public service, there were no doubt those well-practiced in the political art of the two-step avoidance dance in response to constituents' wails of "Can't you do something?!" It seemed the buck never stopped anywhere. Instead, it kept circling endlessly: "Well, unfortunately, there's not a whole lot we can do," "Sorry, but it's not our problem," "You see, it's complicated," "You might give Neighborhood Watch another go," "I suppose you could try suing"…

Beyond the element in local government appearing jaded, hostile or indifferent to Vista's trials and tribulations, it perhaps wasn't so much others not caring as it was that the county's rural population — embracing a relaxed, stand-alone country lifestyle and the time-honored Code of the West championing rugged independence — hadn't an inclination to play cop with fellow residents. They believed people should work out their own problems. Many in government, beyond law enforcement, seemed to lack the disposition one cultivated living in denser, often edgier, urban climates: the willingness to grab the bull by the horns and confront the thorny problems routinely being faced by those living out in the boonies that interfered with the elusive dream of tranquil country living.

That said, the stretched-thin authorities depended on the vast majority of residents to be law-abiding. The largely rural county lacked the funds to enforce its own ordinances if enough for some reason chose to ignore them.

If that happened, it might find itself in deep doo-doo.

CHAPTER 13

Have cookie cutter, will travel

For any whose imagination could take a turn to the surreal, it might've seemed as though the state, in approving such rural subdivisions that each county then oversaw, was perhaps employing social scientists to conduct some weird social lab experiment. As if it wanted to determine how many strangers could live together in the middle of nowhere and deal with a given load of exacting rules and regulations before it drove them all nuts. "Hey guys, I think we might have a new contender...."

People moved to the country for peace and quiet. To enjoy fresh air and live more simply — and be left the hell alone. They no longer wanted to deal with the intrusive bureaucratic mandates of dense city living. Naturally, they did their level best to ignore them here. Even if, in the process, it might've led to unintended consequences... such as an influx of sometimes less-than-law-abiding people, drawn to the wayward place as a promising rural hideout. Some might say the very word 'subdivision' could hinder any such development from thriving, as the word itself sounds so, well... *divisive.*

Historically, when a single party or group founded a settlement, unless it was a boom town, it evolved slowly. There was an organic process at work. New residents experienced a sense of belonging and a measure of empowerment in a slow-growing community where everyone played a vital role and pulled their weight.

Subdivisions not organic

The Vista, in stark contrast, was founded by a realtor who lived 600 miles away. He had every last bit of the land cookie-cutter-platted into 1,641 lots before the first parcel buyer or future resident ever set foot on it. It was his creation, such as it was, at first seeming to aspire to be no more than being a simple shared recreational land where one could enjoy roughing it a few weeks a year.

Then, after a few dozen excited vacationers nurtured a vision and moved onto the land, the lack of infrastructure, fine-tuned growth plans and an unified interest among a majority of lot holders seriously undermined their efforts to maintain the emerging proto-rural village's standard of living. Their approach seemed to have been to play it by ear: "Hey, let's see what we can do here if enough of us get on the same page." Or, again, the possible darker, less altruistic attitude of some might've been more like, "We're going for it, and don't give three hoots in a holler about the rest of the place and their lot owners — beyond any illegal lot occupations and construction that might try to happen, that is."

In any event, nowhere near enough lot owners ever got on the same page. It soon became apparent that members of a wildly diverse ownership, many whose interests and intentions for the parcels seemed at perpetual odds with one another, were more than on different pages or even chapters. They sometimes seemed to be reading entirely different *books*.

Bloom off the rose

Vista's already precarious situation was further complicated after various one-time residents began leasing their homes once the initial bloom of Vista living was off the rose. Lessees, as non-owners, had no say in how the place was run and were ineligible to serve on the board even if they wanted to get involved and help the place along. That is, beyond joining the volunteer fire department, doing fundraisers for it, and spouting off one's two cents' worth at the monthly meetings (if allowed to do so, not being actual property owners).

And again, the place's myriad problems were compounded by the legion of disinterested absentee parcel owners who for ages constituted over 85% of the association membership. They dwarfed the minuscule number of actual residents, yet held equal voting power for any proposal. To many of the purely speculative, the place had become a gone-sour investment that they'd sell the second they got a decent offer. In the meantime, they'd scream and holler over every cent of annual dues increase right along with the few scattered residents, many of whom likewise became indifferent to the outlandish notion of ever lifting a finger (beyond the middle one) to try helping the now-floundering one-time wilderness condo. A place that, seemingly bereft of saving grace, had long ago lost any chance for redemption.

Why bother?

Things had gone wrong so long that many felt there was nothing that could be done but nurse the wobbly operation along the way it was and hope for the best. Long-established residents had their own social scene wired, thank you, and were all too aware how steeply the cards were stacked against the place ever turning itself around. They'd reject as naive and unrealistic the efforts of others to try straightening the place out. Perhaps they even preferred its community-challenged dysfunctionality; no need to try to be sociable with others they often shared little or nothing in common with beyond happening to be living in the same place.

Cynicism ran so deep that hope, like the sad love song, was just another four-letter word.

A prime example of how deeply the lack of civic-mindedness ran: One day in the 1990s, dozens of orange plastic-bagged phone books had been dropped off atop the busy mailbox complex at the Juniper Drive entrance. They were promptly swept to the ground by an irate resident, no doubt taking umbrage at their presence as yet another of the competing local phone books continually being cranked out. They stayed on the ground for *weeks,* like some bizarre avant-garde art installation. While it created an obvious eyesore for everyone who drove by, after more than a month, still no one had addressed it. I didn't live in that part and so held off, waywardly fascinated by such monumental indifference. (Finally, I gathered them up for recycling.)

No doubt many had grumbled to themselves how someone ought to clean them up, but, of course, never thought to be that someone. Disheartened and disgusted by the place's stark dysfunctionality, they might've felt a perverse rush every time they drove past, mentally raking the board over the coals for being so discombobulated that it couldn't (or wouldn't) handle such a simple matter. The place really was like a rural parcels condo, with its overworked one-person road management also expected to keep the common grounds tidy. Not, perish the thought, the detached residents. *Earn your keep, slacker.*

Community center proposal shot down

A more far-reaching example: In 1981, a majority of association members defeated a proposal made by then-board president Eric Prescott. He envisioned the Vista constructing a modest multi-use community center on one of the hundreds of empty lots for the mutual benefit of residents and owner-visitors. The population of the place, then still relatively code-compliant, was growing quickly. It would've meant only a modest extra assessment for two years with the cost spread among many. It could have benefited numerous parcel holders over time, fostering a stronger sense of at least tenuous community by serving as a dedicated, informal space where residents and visitors could meet, exchange information, hold swap meets, brainstorm, coordinate civic activities, and, of course, hold monthly property-owner meetings. By thus making the Vista more livable, it would've surely increased lot values and sales, signaling that the place was finally pulling itself together.

But the sea of terminally disillusioned parcel holders, including, no doubt, many residents themselves, shot the proposal down with mad glee. Blinders firmly in place, they chorused their favorite refrain: "Not One Cent More!"

Telling result: Though Prescott and I moved here at the same time and lived in the same place for decades, we never met.

Many embraced the notion that once they bought the land, except for annual property taxes — some newbie landowners doubtless weren't aware of *that* recurring expense at first — they were home free. Absentee lot holders took strong exception to having to feed the parking meter (as it were) every year for road maintenance on roads they never drove on, lest their property be towed away by the Association through legal repossession for resale to the next, possibly equally clueless buyer.

Sweet someday

Not to paint the situation with too broad a brush… There were also absentee owners who, despite all, continued to treasure the land and its possibilities. They admired and envied those who'd made the bold leap to genteel backwoods living, rooting for them to get the place together. They held wistful hopes that its promising beginnings might yet be rekindled. Some, no doubt, still entertained hopes of moving in and joining their number once the listing ship finally rightsided — or even as-is and hoping for the best. Additionally, a few others continued enjoying their periodic camping retreats on lots farthest from the main traffic arteries and established residences, which were often clustered along the few power lines and within a mile or two of the blacktop.

But such fond sentiments always faced gale-force headwinds of the all-is-futility, deep-entrenched cynicism of other lot holders. They felt stuck with a sucker investment they'd been fool enough to sink their hard-earned money into. And it seemed that most owners — jaded residents and disillusioned absentee owners alike — held scorn for the Pollyanna notion that the place could ever turn itself around. At least, not if it meant prying one more penny from wallet or purse to do so.

Many who wished the place well, but not at their further expense, thought that surely some portion of their annual assessment fee could be allocated to fund any civic improvements community-minded residents might envision. But the yearly budget was always stretched to the limit by the high cost of maintaining the 66 miles of fragile roads. Further depleting available funds, the board repossessed parcels from owners who defaulted, and the association then absorbed its annual county property taxes until new buyers could be found in the super-soft market. Vandalized, damaged and stolen road signs also required frequent replacements. And there were the skyrocketing insurance rates. And thorny legal matters with potential lawsuits, requiring the retention of an expensive attorney. And…

Association manager & board president with conflicts of interest

The professional association manager, hired by the board in the 1980s, was relied upon to handle routine billing, accounting, and budgetary matters, as well as address any legal issues. The association had begun paying the manager's salary once matters became too complex and time-consuming for volunteer board members to handle. Most (including me, years later) were not sufficiently versed in legal matters to grasp the intricate procedures required to run the development (even such as it was) according to Hoyle. Especially not after the state legislature enacted the flurry of new regulations for California subdivisions in 1985 soon known as the Davis-Stirling Act.

It would add insult to injury when one of the salaried managers (the place has had two) — whom residents might reasonably assume would work for the good of the place, it being a nonprofit *public benefit* corporation, and all — brokered lot sales on the side as a real estate agent. In itself, this was perhaps no big deal. But then in 2015 he joined the pumped-up realtors hustling to sell lots to those obviously intent on snapping them up to roll out illicit, scaled pot grows. He, like many, seemed indifferent to the chaos and disruption the sales would unleash on the often laid-back, serene lifestyle that the Vista had, at its best, fitfully enjoyed for decades. (One grower later said, "If they didn't want us growing here, they shouldn't have sold us the lots," showing either a sophistic logic or an apparent moral-cultural disconnect, as if scrambling realtors cared *what* one did with the lots after the sale.)

I doubt if any of the few hundred residents, who had become an unlikely mix of older retired, younger working, and ne'er-do-well hangers-on of all ages, were prepared for what was about to happen… or the fact that our very own association manager, whose salary each lot holder paid towards funding, would actually *help* it happen.

This, perhaps better than anything, illustrates how stupendously upside-down and bass-ackwards the place was. But wait, there was another contender for the dubious distinction of most exploiting the place in brazen self-interest.

Some, maybe even most, volunteer Vista board presidents, themselves residents, tried to keep the well-being of the residency in mind, balanced with the reasonable concerns of the many absentee parcel holders. But one later actually played a central role in the massive realtors' campaign to sell Vista lots to the burgeoning underground grower market. Having ostensibly obtained the file of names and addresses of every lot holder while serving on the board (even then, she was an active realtor, working to move the lots), she and her partner's real estate outfit sent letters and postcards to every single lot holder, inviting them to sell. They knew all too well how many had long felt stuck with unsellable lots and burdened by the annual dues. They pitched something along the good-news lines of, "You might be surprised to know that there are people interested in purchasing your property!"

She and her partner knew most owners would pounce at the chance to finally unload the clunkers and — surprise! — for a tidy sum. "I'll be darned. Harold, it looks like that old place is finally getting popular for some reason, though I can't imagine why." … "That much? Really? Hurry and agree to sell that sorry piece of land before they change their minds."

She had always held that it was the right of each property owner to do with their lot whatever they wanted. "One can cut down every tree on their parcel if they want to," she once opined at a board meeting. In her book, doing whatever one wanted on one's own lot eclipsed any consideration of the community's well-being and the place's overall quality of life, or lack thereof. With such an exploitative mindset, willing to lead the charge in pulling the rug out from under the lives of the place's hundreds of year-round residents, many long established, just to make a fast buck, Vistans would feel like so many pawns on a ruthless, amoral real estate market's chessboard.

Though the development was, again, ostensibly a *non-profit public benefit* corporation, there was so much blatantly *for*-profit, *private* benefit, commodifying, make-money-any-way-you-can-off-the-lame-ass-dead-in-the-water-parcels hustling going on that it beggared belief.

No *there,* there

Many residents had low to no expectations going in. They'd accepted that there wasn't any more *there,* there. Nothing beyond the junipers and sagebrush and simple roads amid a confused mishmash of disparate dwellings and empty lots. Maybe they were even relieved; it suited them fine. Some were only using the place as a temporary perch, ready to move on if and when something better came along.

Many of those the realm eventually attracted indeed seemed far from your conventional sort. They'd dropped anchor here to get as far away from over-complicated, stressful urban forces as possible, yet be not too far from town. They didn't mind a few inconveniences. As one late Section 13 Pilar Road resident, then president of the Siskiyou Arts Council, cheerfully said during a JPR Public Radio interview, "We live out in the middle of nowhere, and we love it!"

Those who had conformed to code requirements, or bought places that had, possessed (at least potentially) the peace of mind to enjoy them for being law-abiding citizens. But even those who hadn't, who were hunkering down hopefully under radar, seemed to feel they had the same inviolable right to enjoy their parcels any way they wanted and not get hassled, while at the same time of course ignoring any laws and ordinances they disapproved of. Human nature could be contrary, perhaps doubly so when living in such a dreamland as the Vista.

Handy place to perch

So it went that the place, a de facto recreational subdivision that failed to segue into a recognized community beyond its fleeting early incarnation, for decades remained an embarrassment of mostly empty lots amid the thinnest scattering of approved residences and an increasing number of unapproved ones.

All the while, it grew an ungovernable spirit.

The situation struck many refugees from urban life as a promising place to land: cheap and remote, but not too remote, with extensive undeveloped acreage all around them. The code-compliant could enjoy simple stand-alone country living, while the non-compliant could often get away with not conforming to code or suffer singed feathers at worst. Both paid the mandatory annual dues (usually) and, as a popular idle pastime, demonized the association board as the source of all evil. With a remarkable shortsightedness that living in the place seemed to foster, it was *the* fly in the ointment interfering with any more carefree country living.

The more cynical among them suspected that the board setup was bogus, probably illegal. Corrupt as hell, anyhow. "Someone oughta sue", "Why I ever moved here...", "This place would be just fine if it weren't for...", "They can't do that, can they?", "This place is friggin' nuts!", ad infinitum. Groundless rumors of corrupt board members misappropriating funds were rampant.

Though such gnarly energies weren't always evident, it could often feel that way. There were, in fact, welcome respites, pleasant lulls when the dread fire-breathing beast of contention slumbered. During such times — especially during gentle springs and early summers — a peaceful, laid-back spirit often prevailed over the land. Despite all, it felt blessed with a rich, restorative tranquility. Polarized energies temporarily checkmated and on the back burner, grateful denizens relished the serenity.

Such idyllic periods, alas, seldom seemed to last long.

CHAPTER 14

The Intolerant Years: Mid-1970s through mid-1990s

While there was something to be said for the place making everyone feel like a king or queen of their own mini kingdom, their own little backwoods hideaway bought for a song, one had to keep tuning out the perennial joker in the deck: the endless battles over code compliance. It could make the less affluent and nonconforming feel more like serfs living under the yoke of the overlords who'd met legal residency requirements and were determined to keep them enforced by any means short of armed vigilantism. Sometimes they succeeded; other times they came off like so many bumbling Barney Fifes.

This joker in the deck, like a rude Jack-in-the-box, kept popping up to put a crimp in the lives of non-compliant dwellers during the Intolerant Years, which roughly spanned between the mid-1970s and mid-1990s. As mentioned, domains farthest from the blacktop often had so few others living anywhere near that inhabitants might've imagined their digs more like pioneer homesteads of yore rather than any dratted modern-day sub-division parcels subject to a slew of nit-picky, spirit-stifling rules and regulations. But even then, the latter reality usu-ally asserted itself sooner or later to put a damper on one's day.

Some (certainly not all) board members and their cohorts of that period — fondest hopes for the place fading into obliv-ion and, consequently, minds bent into pretzels — went on raging mad drunks with the power being a board member seemed to confer. They ran about like so many little T. rexes. With barred teeth and razor claws, the uber law-and-order champions wielded ruthless authority over the rabble... or tried to. They were dead-set on salvaging what they could of their once-secret retirement hideaway, in the process becom-ing out-and-out authoritarians and making the place akin to Dante's fifth ring of Hell, the Circle of Wrath. No doubt they felt their violent emotion and extreme-mindset behavior were justified; the only alternative was to stand by and watch their sweet dream circle the drain in numb disbelief.

Fast-forward, and board members, though still grumbling over the rampant non-compliance ruining their property values and quality of life, seemed to have gradually become resigned to what time had proven to be an unsolvable problem. Board meeting members and attendees, many mindful of the ephem-erally idyllic times of yore, at some point sank into a collectively depressed, *what's-the-use?* state of mind.

Perhaps it wasn't surprising that inertia prevailed even as their once-iron authority began rusting away. Residents of a place so long paralyzed by ceaseless discord still somehow felt they couldn't do diddly-squat without first getting the board's approval — and then grow old waiting for it. "Matter tabled til next meeting [yawn] … motion for adjournment?"

The same thing happened if one wanted to start up an official volunteer effort to help the place along.

Beleaguered crew aboard the foundering *HMS Vista*

One day at a monthly meeting held in then-president Bonnie Jolly's living room, I volunteered to become the subdivision's unpaid custodian. With even a little real encouragement from them, I was psyched to tackle the epidemic of road litter and windblown detritus often despoiling the otherwise scenic wooded roadways. They apparently thought it a good idea and duly voted me into the new position. But it was an unreal experience: It was almost as if they'd approved the post in their sleep. They didn't bother to address any details the position might require — supplying trash bags, gas allowance, or reimbursing for dump fees — nothing. (I hadn't thought to bring such matters up, either.) So I quit my official post before I started, knowing I needn't say anything to anyone.

Their hearts simply weren't into such things. Burned out from thankless volunteering, accustomed to receiving only grief for their efforts and depressed over the sorry state of affairs in general, they were coasting on autopilot. They could muster only enough energy to cover essential routine matters like road maintenance. (I'd continue gathering road litter informally, as did a few others, likewise concerned.)

With the way board members often seemed to go through the motions so woodenly, calling it in, other residents, knowing the beast was losing its teeth, began tackling things as they saw fit without seeking the board's permission. Things like setting aright a road sign that had been run into and was precariously listing or had fallen over, or repairing a stretch of road in front of one's place rather than going through stupefyingly sluggish official channels.

Apathy and a sense of hopelessness in the place were so chronic and entrenched, we were like a beleaguered crew aboard a foundering ship: We lacked the will to do anything more than bail just enough water to keep from going under.

What rules?

Jumping back to the earlier Intolerant Years… Despite a seemingly bonkers board throwing its weight around while on nearly constant red alert, the remote circumstances still somehow lent a tenuous assurance that, even then, one could (or should) be able to do whatever they wanted to on their own land. No uptight board — lacking credibility and legal enforcement powers, and gradually receiving less support and cooperation from county authorities — could stop them, no matter how much ruckus they might raise.

Private-property rights were sacrosanct, after all. The more rebellious and independent-thinking dwellers shut out the reality of being subject to the rules and regulations of the external world, especially as championed by a self-important, busybody board of infernally meddling "directors." It didn't register as something needed in the simple rustic realm. It was too invasive, too alien, too self-defeating to the very reason people moved here.

At the risk of overstressing the point, the illusion of anything-goes manifested largely because the vast majority of parcel owners were detached investors who lived far off and rarely, if ever, visited their lots. To actual dwellers, they held no more than an easily tuned-out phantom presence. Longtime residents like me came to view the 1,000-plus vacant, undeveloped, unsellable parcels almost as a de facto permanent park commons. As a result, some could feel like stewards not only of their own mini-fiefdoms of two to three acres, but also of the luxuriant buffer zones of dozens, even scores, of empty parcels.

It could make one feel land-rich indeed.

Silver lining: A nudist paradise

This reality often created conditions so isolated — nobody around to say boo — that certain social norms, even deeply entrenched ones like mandatory dress beyond the privacy of one's home, easily faded over time. I was one of a handful living in Vista's more remote reaches, surrounded by *hundreds* of undeveloped, unfenced wooded lots. Anyone with even a whisper of an inner bohemian could, if they felt like it, stroll about their land buck naked all day long in nicest weather. There was next to no chance of being caught out of uniform, as it were.

One had the rare opportunity to enjoy that indescribably delicious rush of feeling an intimate oneness with the elements. Often, no vehicles drove on the furthest back roads for weeks at a time. And almost no one else ever walked anywhere (perhaps a legacy of most founders being from the uber-car-centric L.A. area).

Such remote conditions often inspired more than a few freer-spirited Vistan denizens to enjoy going nekkid as jays all day long, sometimes even for days at a time, whether at home, outdoors on one's property, or sometimes freehiking through adjacent uninhabited areas, which could feel like enchanted wildwood nude. Harmful ultraviolet rays weren't so intense then, so one could often embrace sunshine as a healing balm and experience an almost supernatural high enjoying the day free of man-made cover-ups.

One hot, sleepy summer day in the early 2000s, when what few people lived here then had either driven to a lake to cool down, gone to the coast, or were glued in front of their TVs, AC blasting and cold beer in hand, I thought of an easy way to cool off. Not wearing a stitch, I hiked a mile downhill over BLM land to enjoy immersing in Whitney Creek's land-trapped snow melt, then pooling along Buck Horn Road. I wore only flip-flops (with cotton shorts slung over my shoulder in case I needed to cover up). I skinny-dipped to my heart's content there, in a cool, deliciously silky-soft, silt-bottomed pool that stretched some 50 yards. A tall earthen berm stood between it and the adjacent road, providing privacy from any passing traffic (none passed). After gathering a few pumice stones the creek always washed down Mt. Shasta in summer, for my thriving home business, I leisurely hiked back home, never having needed to cover during the entire adventure.

Such were the exhilarating and liberating experiences one might enjoy here. Other free-minded spirits did similar free-hiking along other creek stretches. You could indulge your sensuous nature in exotic weather that begged to be enjoyed without needless apparel interfering with communing with nature. How many places could you do that, other than a naturist resort or free beach? Obviously, one of the advantages of the Vista being such a failed rural subdivision was that it was a nudist paradise.

By the year 2000, at age 50, I'd become so convinced of the therapeutic value of mindful nudity for easily, rapidly reintegrating body, mind and spirit on new levels that I (lowkeyly) advocated for changing the staid mandatory cover-up policy at nearby Stewart Mineral Springs resort, where I volunteered. After convincing management it was time to align with the open-minded policies of the more popular rural mineral springs resorts in the wider region, like Harbin, Jackson Wellsprings, Wilbur, Orr and Breitenbush, and go clothing-optional, the place suddenly felt liberated. Untold thousands, some undoubtedly for the first time since toddlerhood, enjoyed public skinny-dipping, sunbathing au naturel, and nude saunas over the next 17 years. And they had the magical earth medicine of Mt. Shasta Vista's land to thank for having inspired me to advocate for the new policy. (The change *might've* happened eventually anyhow, but I liked to think I made sure it happened sooner rather than later.)

Who's minding the place?

Some residents, beyond board members in contact with the absentee owners, might've vaguely sensed their displeasure with the sorry state of the place. It was indeed disheartening. It enabled firewood-selling tree poachers to raid the unfenced lots of absentees at will. Sometimes, parcels and adjacent forestry land harbored actual squatters. And off-roaders tore through absentee owners' usually unposted, unfenced, undeveloped parcels with impunity.

Though perhaps having no one to blame but themselves for being dumb enough to buy into what was such a colossal developmental misfire, it was easier to blame the residency and the mostly powerless board, who together sometimes gave the impression they didn't care. (And indeed, some, only trying to make the best of a bad situation for a while, actually didn't care a whole lot.)

Others tried to make a difference. While out one day gathering pumice stones along a remote stretch of Whitney Creek below Highway 97, I ran into a new board member, a Mr. Arbuckle. He was busy moving boulders to divert the creek's flow from moving down alongside Buck Horn Road to a better-bermed route just beyond Rising Hill Road. He admitted he hadn't gotten permission from the forestry service. I didn't begrudge him that; I found it encouraging to see someone actually rolling up their sleeves and doing what needed to be done to try to help the place along.

Whether one sensed the absent owners' general displeasure or not, it was definitely a subtle yet pernicious force. Their collective ire over the pitiful state of affairs was part and parcel of the overload of corrosive influences at work. It could gnaw at one's peace of mind — if only vaguely and on the unconscious level — right along with the in-your-face code-compliant dwellers waging war on the non-compliant and dealing with water scarcity. One might even say that the huge absentee ownership was in a way responsible for the place never mustering enough public-spirited concern to help itself out of its dire straits. Not even enough to vote for a modest community center. If not *the* straw that broke the camel's back, it was definitely a serious contender.

Early pot growing inside an intractable tract

In the early 2000s, one of the few residents then furtively growing small patches of illicit cannabis — long before California's changing pot laws decriminalized such once-nefarious doings — found himself with new neighbors. A couple seemed determined to do the exact same thing. Wanting to avoid increasing the possibility of bringing unwanted attention to his own clandestine operation, he confronted them, persuading them to leave by threatening violence in no uncertain terms if they didn't.

A very few others were also discreetly growing a few pot plants outdoors by then (plus maybe one or two growing indoors with lights), mostly for their own enjoyment, but sometimes also to generate some extra income. The place had a sunny, dry climate (if not ideal soil) and was remote enough to pursue such cultivation without getting hassled *if* one kept their operation low-key.

The Vista's early verboten pot grows, limited as they were, would naturally help set the stage for later, larger-scale illicit cultivation, showing yet again how the remote place was an irresistible draw for all kinds of people for all sorts of reasons.

Changing pot laws

California, of course, had legalized medical marijuana in 1996, the first in the nation to do so. Then, in the years preceding recreational pot legalization by voters in late 2016, 20 long years later, a few enterprising Vistan residents began pooling together scrip from the sea of registered, mostly sham medical-marijuana "patients." ("I can't sleep at night, Doc" … "Well, slip me a Benjamin and your troubles are over.") It entitled them to grow six plants per person per year. In effect, they could grow up to 99 plants and ostensibly supply 16 so-called patients, while still technically complying with state law and avoiding unwelcome federal interest for growing one more. As time went by, enforcement of such ostensible medicinal grows grew pretty lax.

After 2016 and California's legalization of recreational cannabis, the 99-plant figure reportedly soon became the tacitly agreed-upon limit, barring official complaints, for the by-then-overwhelmed Siskiyou County authorities, scrip paperwork or not. The state's six-plant limit for private individuals growing at their own residences for personal use applied to all but *licensed* commercial cultivators. In time, it would be boldly ignored as all but unenforceable.

Vigilante episodes

Between a critical handful of the more defiant, ignoring any rules and regulations interfering with doing whatever the heck one wanted; a county seemingly throwing up its hands and abandoning the place as a hopeless mess, actually scrapping its residency-code enforcer post for several critical years; and radically changing times in general — between these, respect for the rule of law in the Vista got on some shaky ground.

A few more examples will show how shaky.

As mentioned, some less than civic-minded entrepreneurial residents (as well as invading outsiders) routinely poached trees on empty lots and adjacent forestry land to buck into rounds, split, and sell for firewood. They felled scores of standing snags, sometimes even living trees, including some of the few tall pines that had long graced the Vista, leaving behind unsightly stumps and slash piles on the long-undisturbed land. The Shasta-Trinity National Forest's law enforcement officer once showed me a regional map on his office wall; it was covered with what must have been over 1,000 tiny red dots, each representing an illegal cut.

Another party set up a large dog-rescue kennel on an unimproved, mostly treeless parcel in Section 21; neighbors up to a half-mile away were forced to endure the endless barking of dozens of unhappily caged residents, sometimes left in the hot sun, for over a year, until the operation was finally shut down.

Bolder souls

Bolder souls took the law into their own hands. When a resident at the top of White Drive discovered that the surveyor ages back had erred in his lot boundaries, he tried to close off the major through-road running past his place. He erected a padlocked gate across it, even though it was ages too late to legally remedy the miscalculation. A young, devil-may-care neighbor on Meadow Road, Billy Bracken, regularly used the road; he didn't think twice when he encountered the sudden barrier: He backed up his bad-boy truck, gunned the engine, and smashed through the gate, end of problem.

And a neighbor on McClarty Road was furious over how two young men routinely roared by his place twice a day, making a racket and raising clouds of dust, just to needle him because he'd mocked them for being gay. One evening, he furtively dug a slanted trench across the road. That night, they sped by at their usual time, promptly lost control, and ran into a tree. As they staggered back, shaken and furious, to confront him, he proved to be even madder: He shot at them. (Fortunately, he missed and was later arrested.)

On another occasion, a resident on Cardinal Road saw red when he learned that a scuzzy new neighbor had tried hitting on his young teen daughter. Along with a wrecking crew he rounded up, he descended on the culprit's land late one night when they knew he was on vacation in the county lockup and vandalized and looted the place to a fare-thee-well.

And when a Black man briefly occupied a vacant stone cottage on McLarty Road and was discovered one night by its absentee owner, the latter held a shotgun on him for a half-hour until the sheriff deputy arrived. (A while later, I saw the owner in town the day after the first-ever person of African ancestry got voted into the White House; he held a look of stunned disbelief and utter loathing.)

Multiply this knowledge of the goings on in my own section times seven for the other sections, each with doubtless similar histories of edgy incidents over time, and there was indeed trouble in River City.

Obviously, the place's auspicious start during simpler times — its upbeat, if convention-locked, law-abiding dwellers, experiencing euphoric bonhomie camping together, then settling the land — was ancient history. It was the quaint way of life of a misty bygone era, blasted to smithereens ages ago.

CHAPTER 15

Blame it on the mountain

One could maybe blame the mountain and its powerful energy, at least in part, for Vista's residents not working together any better. Some hold that its emanations stimulate one's upper-body energy chakras. While initially revving the imagination, it can also pull one meditatively inward. Bolstered by Mt. Shasta Vista's founder, who, as an enthusiastic fellow camper in the early years, championed the freedom to do whatever one wanted on their parcels (within the existing norms of propriety, of course), the mountain's influence might've indeed worked to make one feel like one's lot was akin to Superman's impregnable Fortress of Solitude.

Brief competing for board membership

Long after the honeymoon camping period and early home-steading years had ended and more newcomers settled in without county blessing, people actually competed to get voted onto the board for a while. Some no doubt hoped to mellow the place, willing to look the other way about the all-but-unenforceable county ordinances being ignored, so long as residents otherwise remained peaceable. They hoped to make the best of a bad situation. Others, bearing no such live-and-let-live inclinations, kept grinding the code enforcement ax. They were bound and determined to keep alive the increasingly toothless hardline campaign against unsanctioned dwellings, their dwellers, and pretty much anyone who even looked at them cross-eyed.

That peculiar, relatively community-active period passed soon enough. Fast-forward a decade, and the place was so overwhelmed by openly non-compliant, sometimes hostile, *what's-it-to-you?* dwellers, that the situation seemed hopeless. A marked air of civic indifference had emerged. The ungovernable atmosphere, aggravated by and reflecting the 1990s' spiking national crime rate, was punctuated by the helpless wails of long-suffering compliant residents: "What's *happening* to this place?"

We seemed lost in a fog, a ship at sea without sail or rudder, aimlessly adrift. "Water, water, everywhere / nor any drop to drink."

Rambunctious Whitney Creek
and a Forest Service lawsuit

Ironically, residents of water-parched lands sometimes needed to scramble to keep water *out*. Silty snow melt poured in from next door's seasonally running Whitney Creek whenever it decided to go on a rampage. It periodically flooded areas of the adjacent Section 28's lowlands at Buck Horn Road or Rising

Hill Road, depending on the part-time creek's changing course. In the eighties, after years of silt-laden waters and mud flows wreaking havoc with vulnerable roads and eroding private parcels, the association, led by then-president Eric Prescott, sued the U.S. Forest Service. They'd allowed the course of the creek — actually a seasonal snow-melt wash — to be diverted directly towards our new subdivision by removing a dam built above State Highway 97 by parties in the area who owned what later became Lake Shastina and no longer needed it.

Our association won the suit. The $250,000 settlement funded the creation of the massive earthen berms still in place and maintained along Buck Horn Road and what's left of Rising Hill Road, protecting the area from future flooding. Between annual bulldozing efforts to repair the latest erosion from the previous year's water action and the creek sometimes cutting new courses through the dried silt or mud, the waters have mostly been kept safely out of harm's way.

But not always. In August 2022, floodwaters and a massive mud flow again breached the Buck Horn berm. After prolonged 100-degree-plus weather had generated extraordinary amounts of snow and glacier melt, possibly building up behind an ice dam far up-mountain before bursting, the land was inundated on both sides of the berm, prompting a Code Red evacuation alert. Afterwards, some of the by-then-ubiquitous grow sites located there looked like eerie, mud-caked artifacts of a bygone civilization.

—◦✕◦—

Bored writer joins the board

In 2013, after over 30 years of myself feeling little fondness for the board — at times being demonized by certain of its members in return, short fuses being in good supply all around — I up and joined it. At the time, board volunteering had hit an all-time low. It was hard-pressed to fill more than three of its five seats, the minimum required for a legal quorum to conduct essential business like approving new road maintenance outlays.

They weren't too picky about who volunteered. One only needed to be a code-compliant resident or absentee owner in good standing. If not rallying, the place could conceivably go into dread state receivership as a failed subdivision and face unpleasant and costly consequences. As one of the few who even sporadically attended monthly meetings, I got roped into serving as secretary one evening in 2012, by then-president and fellow longtime resident Pamela Simpson, before I knew it.

While it turned out the development's actual defaulting never posed an imminent threat, at times it did seem to flirt with such an ignominious fate. It felt like no one cared *what* happened to the poor, misbegotten place. Indeed, few seemed to appreciate how various residents volunteered their time to serve as members and meet the state's mandate and do what needed to be done to maintain at least a semblance of functionality. For their troubles, the volunteers were, as said, routinely vilified as power-crazed busybodies (a lingering attitude from the Intolerant Years). They were mindlessly interfering with other residents' would-be tranquility. After I joined, my non-compliant neighbor acquaintances became a bit more guarded around me, as if I'd possibly gone over to the dark side.

With so many members — absent lot holders included — routinely damning the board, or at least being supremely indifferent to it, all but its more determined and thicker-skinned members soon burned out from serving on it; they were variously overwhelmed, jaded, embittered, bored and discouraged in record time. Those who hung in there often could appear like charred remnants of their former selves. Some were like dogs with a bone, determined not to let go of the reins for fear no one else could do the job. One longtime treasurer, Alfo Baldwin, owned some eight parcels. He always strongly opposed increasing the annual lot assessment even though the budget was hemorrhaging. The obvious conflict of interest was apparently never considered important enough to even bring up.

Indeed, from time to time, the board seemed to attract would-be volunteers with private agendas up their sleeves. One, before his tenure got abruptly cut short, had provoked a violent incident with the road manager because he didn't want his road frontage worked on. Others seemed only to be seeking the dubious prestige and sense of entitlement board membership might confer without having to do any actual work.

Soul-crushing boredom

As I was to learn first-hand, the board's pressure-cooker meetings could easily undermine one's sometimes-tenuous peace of mind. One had to be in full psychic armor, ready for battle if, say, an outraged resident or visiting owner attended, sitting there glaring like a ticking time bomb until given the allotted three minutes to vent their spleen. Or, more often the case, one was forced to endure soul-crushing boredom under cold fluorescent lighting. Or be made to do the dirty work if the manager told you and others to, say, sign stacks of legal foreclosure papers for property owners who had either given up on the place, were in dire financial straits, or both.

One struggled to rise above the sea of paperwork and the dry, formal meeting procedure, endured in the cramped, chilly, fire station backroom, if ever hoping to accomplish anything one might conceivably be proud of. Spirits were often so subdued that it could feel like we were in some clinical group depression. As if everyone felt the thankless grand futility of it all but plugged away anyhow out of a misguided sense of civic duty. After serving 18 months, my replacement tenure on the board was set to expire with the upcoming election. Another board member put my name on the ballot without even asking if I wanted to run. Predictably, I was burned out by then and so declined to serve further, even though elected.

Over time, the development occasionally seemed to be getting back on track (as much as any track existed) under the guidance of the more capable, on-the-ball, open-minded board members. They scrambled to get the place up to speed after tackling remedial catch-up chores. Then it would derail all over again with the endless shuffle of new volunteers, sometimes less motivated or knowledgeable, coming on board. There was always a lot of slow-on-the-job orientation and a steep learning curve. By the time new board members began to get a tenuous grasp of procedures and current issues, they were already burned out or bored silly. And so the learning process started again with other newbies from an ever-shrinking pool of willing resident volunteers of good standing.

A diverting contest

No doubt, like countless well-meaning board members before and after me, I'd hoped to turn the place around: Crusader Rabbit to the rescue. The situation just seemed so ridiculously depressing, so needlessly downbeat, so absurdly all-is-futility-so-why-even-bother, that surely it couldn't take too much effort to reverse such a dispiriting downward spiral.

You'd've thunk.

A writing enthusiast, I penned many features and editorials for the *Vistascope* newsletter. I briefly took heart after launching a contest with small cash prizes I donated, challenging readers to come up with funny or thoughtful new spell-outs for the Mt. Shasta Vista Property Owners Association's acronym, MSVPOA. Several responded. The winners:

- **Majestic Sandy Volcanic Paradise in Outback America** (Pam Schifano)

- **Most Sacred Vacation Place Of All** (John Underhill)

- **Mountain Steaming, Vacate Property on A-12** (Sandy Honeyball-Berry)

All is futile... born under a dark star?

But despite such fun diversions, I struck out, just like everyone else. It appeared far too late to change the course of the place's wonky, generations-old trajectory. The beleaguered ship Vista had by then not only left the dock but sailed halfway around the world and was floundering in unknown waters. The die was cast, the dismal course set. Barring a miracle, it was wishful thinking to think that concerned board members could ever pull the place out of the quagmire it had been so helplessly stuck in for so long.

We were dinosaurs, floundering in a tar pit, lamenting our bleak fate.

Though various mindful visitors over time often sensed the land's at times notable serenity — some overnight visitors reported having the best dreams of their lives here — cynics, not without reason, came to dismiss the troubled realm out of hand: "No water, no trees, nothing but desert and rattlesnakes; it's a friggin' wasteland, I tell ya." To them, it was just a sketchy de facto substandard rural bedroom community; a hideout for hard-drinking loners, small-time growers and spaced-out nature freaks; maybe a few respectable, hardworking residents hoping to play out the elusive dream of idyllic country living and obviously having picked the wrong place.

The way so many routinely slammed the place, one might've concluded that it was born under a dark star, some wicked witch's cauldron boiling over with loathsome ingredients, any effort to avoid its sorrowful fate folly.

Resistance was futile.

A dollop of esoterica: Vista's astrology chart and cardology fortune

Some might be curious to know the celestial forces in play on November 3, 1965, the day the place legally came into being. The calendar date was shared by TV's Rosanne Barr, football's Collin Kaepernick and actor Charles Bronson. One might say the resulting early Scorpio, brooding, super-wound energies imprinted on the development at formation guaranteed that the place would always be more than a tad on the intense side.

Lightening things, Mars and Venus were loosely conjunct in nature-loving Sagittarius, along with the place having a compassionate, dreamy Pisces moon. But then, Jupiter was retrograde, potentially making it hard to find meaningful direction. Saturn was also retrograde. According to Vedic astrologer Nidhi Trivedi, this placement tends "… to instill a serious attitude towards life, emphasizing discipline and responsibility. The placement can lead to a strict or overly demanding nature, resulting in challenges related to authority and self-worth."

Challenges with authority, yup.

Then, related, there's cardology — the study of planetary influences thought to form a unique DNA signature for each day of the year — symbolized by its corresponding playing card (some days share the same card, but each has unique meaning). The Vista's 4 of diamonds birthday, according to the book *Cards of Destiny* by Sharon Jeffers, created an "innate restlessness, possible dissatisfaction with what one was doing," and could make one "… *a dreamer who doesn't always allow dreams to become reality* [italics added]."

That last surely fit the Vista to a T. It was a dreamland through and through. And its denizens often seemed unable to manifest their happy visions in waking state.

—◦◦✕◦◦—

Perfect storm

Somewhere along the way, the once openly shared, carefree vacation land had reached a critical tipping point. Beyond it, anarchistic-leaning residents were increasingly emboldened to do their own thing, lawful or not, while hundreds of absentee landholders, filled with buyer's remorse, had little or no interest in the dratted place except to cash out the first chance they got.

Most would-be residents had long lost any inclination to build to code. One contractor, who in later years appeared to have built a two-story house up to snuff on Catherine Road minus a well, electrical hookup, and possibly a septic system, would deprive the county of the opportunity to give its official blessing. Why bother? The county had dropped its residential code-enforcement position by then, and a fully compliant place wouldn't fetch enough return to justify the added expense of a deep well and extended power lines if sold, given how it was located in such a squirrelly mishmash of a place.

Countless daunting factors had been piling up for decades. Combined with changing external realities, the place's conditions appeared to be shaping into a perfect storm.

Circumstances already let any so inclined have a field day pursuing whatever dubious land uses they might conjure — junkyards, dog kennels, probably meth labs — for being on such remote, private dirt roads tucked away from all but the prying eyes of a few nosy neighbors who seemed powerless to do anything about it anyway. It didn't seem to matter that such dubious land uses upset the tranquility for which the code-compliant dropped anchor here and built sweat equity in establishing their places, or had bought places from those who had and paid accordingly.

The subdivision, long ago given up as a lost cause by the county, residents and absentee lot holders alike, was the very poster child of a failed subdivision. Meanwhile, more and more denizens of the terminally wayward realm belted out rousing choruses of Cole Porter's "Anything Goes."

Without any better harmonizing force — one with at least a semblance of proactive community concern and respect for the rule of law — a disorderly spirit quickly gained an outsized influence. It seemed the majority of less-vested residents were so used to the place being intractably dysfunctional — a quirky, cheap, low-key hideaway with a powerless board and often unresponsive county authorities — that they couldn't be bothered to read the writing on the wall. Or read it and felt nothing could be done.

One didn't need the omniscience of 20-20 hindsight to realize that by the early 2010s two things had become clear: (1) The Vista was a rudderless ship, vulnerable to drifting into potentially perilous straits, and (2) its hinterland residents either didn't care or felt helpless to do anything to try preserving what was, despite all, a fitfully tranquil rural lifestyle, one now duly taken for granted.

The place was thus leaving the door wide open for even greater misadventures to occur.

CHAPTER 16

It's the water

Knowing where the Vista was coming could go a long way towards understanding where it was headed. Was the place's metaphorical foundation (as it were) only coming full circle? First, it was trailers set on sand, then conventional homes built on rock, then more trailers set on sand.

Whatever happened or would happen, lack of water always played a big role. As Klamath River County Estates (KRCE) landowner Will Jensen noted in long-ago blogging about his exhaustive search to find the ideal affordable rural home property with an inspiring Mt. Shasta view, "No matter who we talked to, we were warned away from Mt. Shasta Vista … we were told repeatedly that Mt. Shasta Vista was bad for wells."

Hoping to remedy the chronic water shortage in the early 2000s, a few solution-minded residents applied for a government grant to fund a proposed centralized water distribution system. It was rejected, deemed too costly and labor-intensive a project to help too few.

The realm's need for dependable water was highlighted by its arid high-desert land — usually baking hot and bone dry in summer — and further aggravated by its volcanic terrain that baffles geohydrologists. The terrain often made hitting water through lava strata and voids touch-and-go. And even when successful, the water might be undrinkable without treatment for suspended volcanic minerals.

An early owner couple drilling for water apparently hit a lava tube. They felt a steady, cool stream of air flowing up from the ground. After sinking a well elsewhere and building their home, they installed a fan and ductwork to harness the cold air stream and naturally air-conditioned their new place.

Those who had wells often had vegetable gardens. One resident, Chris Burns, on Eagle Road in Section 7, was a serious farmer. While the soil in the Vista is sandy and not optimal for growing food, he soon remedied that. He set up a diversion program with Mt. Shasta's landfill management, regularly hauling home trailers full of yard clippings and other compostable yard waste and working it into the soil. With goats further breaking down the waste and fertilizing the land, he soon had bumper crops of dozens of different foodstuffs, including 20 pounds of garlic the year I visited.

Back to the '80s: Country roads weren't accepted

By the mid-1980s, the Vista had grown to about 150-200 residences with wildly varying degrees of ambition and code compliance. Scattered over nearly seven square miles, it was still only a relative sprinkling.

It appeared that many new city-centric owners were averse to driving on unpaved roads. They never learned to accept and respect the place's cinder-surfaced thoroughfares for the honest country roads they were. Upset for having to drive so slowly over them, in the process getting their nice, shiny vehicles all dusty and ruining the latest car wash, they found it intolerable to endure up to five miles over the sometimes narrow, winding cinder roads to reach a property. A half mile of unpaved road was more than enough for anyone to have to endure.

For them, the desire for rural seclusion was weighed against the desire for easy in and out. One might say such people were only flirting with country living. Some residents appeared to dislike the roads so much that at one point they actually proposed paving them. They'd cover the prohibitive cost by special assessments (as did not-too-distant Shasta Forest development, over time), which the sea of absentee lot owners would then of course disproportionately shoulder. The proposal was a nonstarter: It would never have received the required two-thirds vote. Apparently, they'd thought the cinder roads were the most pressing problem holding the place back. Their heads were so stuck in city ways, they couldn't appreciate how the lack of paved roads were perhaps the least of the place's shortcomings.

And *was* it even a shortcoming? With so many of the deemed less-desirable parcels scattered deep in the hinterlands, again, it lent such regions a profoundly tranquil, untamed, park-like ambiance to be savored by anyone willing to go the distance and embrace country living rather than merely tolerate it.

But it often felt that, no matter how much pristine land one might enjoy, a foreboding undercurrent always lurked just below the surface. One that could seriously jam one's peace of mind and ability to more than fitfully enjoy the oft-heralded joys of country living. Between the regional community that never accepted the place or wished it well, and the resolve of code-compliant residents to battle the insufferable code scoffers dragging down the place and property values, it felt like one was always waiting for the other shoe to drop. Even if a resident was compliant, an almost palpable tension often filled the air. On the subtle plane, it was like living in a crowded tenement, angry landlord pounding on the door.

This was one of the grand ironies of living in the Vista. Either you detached and became philosophical about it all, or you perhaps soon found yourself over-identifying with artist Munch's screamer.

It would drive more than a few to drink.

Missing word sank efforts

Around 2012, a handful of the more civic-minded residents launched a long-overdue effort. A committee was formed to try to revise the woefully outdated and sketchy CC&Rs. Not over-haul them outright, but at least tinker a bit around the edges to make them a bit more relevant to current realities. After much slow sledding, a glitch in the progress report, printed and sent to every owner, derailed efforts. The pamphlet cover's title was supposed to read: "Proposed Changes to Mt. Shasta

Vista Bylaws." But the critical first word, *Proposed,* had been omitted, making the changes sound like a done deal.

This prompted a barely peaceable pitchforks-and-torches crowd to storm the next board meeting. Residents who usually avoided meetings like the plague were coming out of the woodwork. They were all but convinced the power-mad board was staging a coup.

The long and winding roads; Whitney Creek revisited

While you had your own private parcel, the modest annual road dues assessments, often resented, were frequently contested by residents if not getting their own roads better maintained. Various absentee owners added to the chorus, claiming they could barely reach their parcels if they were located on the least-populated back roads. Some of these roads didn't get touched for years. Some, like the roughly 200 acres north of me, weren't worked for over a decade. The most neglected stretches had sagebrush crowding the roadway. Plus, they might develop deep, dry pools of tire-grabbing, quicksand-like silt so treacherous that AAA tow trucks eventually refused to come out to rescue trapped members' vehicles, after once getting their own rig stuck and, in turn, having to call in a monster tow truck to rescue the rescuer.

It didn't help matters that our part-time neighbor, Whitney Creek, could get rambunctious when summer temperatures climbed above 100 degrees F. The product of the mountain's often heavy winter snowpack and melting glaciers, the surging melt could cut new courses and work its way through the earthen berms.

It once submerged much of Section 28 under nine inches of water, necessitating an evacuation and making regional TV news. The place's oldest longtime resident and native Arkansan, Bill Waterson, hyucked for the camera, finding it all amusing. This was perhaps because, as a resident since the early 1970s, he knew the place had a wayward talent for attracting disasters. (The man was a paradox: Though having a conspicuous redneck streak, his grandson told me he'd smoked pot since he was 13; this explained why he found so many things amusing. He was undoubtedly the Vista's first and by far oldest redneck hippie.)

The worst of many floods over time until the massive earthen berm was built, the flood washed away some roads so thoroughly that the board ultimately abandoned them after buying up the parcels of those who couldn't reach them short of driving a Hummer. Members figured it was cheaper in the long run than rebuilding the periodically washed-out, little-used road stretches.

Most of a road vanishes

After one notable flood along the southernmost east-west road in the Vista, three-fourths of Rising Hill Road vanished and wasn't rebuilt. For ages after, delivery people and first-timers used outdated maps or relied on Google Maps, both of which were misleading and got them majorly disoriented, if not hopelessly stuck, trying to turn around at sudden dead ends; they were looking for roads that no longer existed.

And they drove on roads no longer maintained. One time I caught up with a UPS driver who'd relied on an obsolete map showing a hillside road connecting two of our mile-separate sections via Country Road to Thrush Road over neglected BLM land. The board had briefly maintained the road, but then decided to discontinue because it wasn't association property. The road soon suffered extensive erosion from rainfall over long, steep stretches. The delivery person, relying on a faulty map, had barely managed to traverse it; he appeared amazed he'd successfully run the gantlet.

Roads destroyed by creek floods also routinely waylaid unwary drivers. Finally, the association — decades after there'd arisen an obvious need for them — installed signs at the front of the dead-end roads. And the earthen berm built up on Buck Horn Road at Country discouraged use of the increasingly sketchy hillside shortcut road. For a while, it seemed the only ones still using it were sticky-fingered "salvagers", who, back-roads savvy, nimbly traversed it in their old, beat-up, high-clearance pickups. They'd sneak into the higher section's back entrance in the dead of night — sometimes even broad daylight — to peruse the current pickings on what were deemed abandoned properties and so fair game for salvaging in their universe.

Veritable train wreck of a place

Vistan parcel holders were, by and large, a frugal lot: bought the land cheap, moved in cheap, wanted to keep things cheap. They often harbored strong stand-alone tendencies, or they fell into them over time as a matter of course. It seemed futile to try to rally any community awareness and cooperation in a place that increasingly harbored such an ornery, "Leave me alone and we'll get along fine" attitude.

Yet again, the situation was compounded by that sea of absentee owners who'd only bought parcels as speculative investments and came to regard their unsellable holdings as a bane in their lives. The widespread disenchantment and indifference of the majority of lot owners, resident and absent alike, was guaranteed to arrest any errant inclination one might've felt to try rescuing the wayward realm with its seeming talent for hopeless discombobulation.

At some point, lacking any solid foundation on which to sustain and build a recognized community, the Vista had been overwhelmed by adverse circumstances and short-circuited. The place became the arrested development that first-time visitors routinely dropped their jaws over. Such a "left for dead" train wreck of a place set amid an otherwise seemingly peaceful and scenic backwoods seemed unreal. It was as if a long-abandoned film set for a low-budget Western was left to gather mothballs in a studio's outdoor lot. Or it was a place that had grown too big for its britches, trying to rise above its lowly station, and was now paying the price for its rank impertinence.

The earliest settlers who built their code-approved homes surely realized that everyone would have to comply with health and building regulations if the development were to remain a respectable fledgling community. But, of course, people, not caring what they thought, swooped in on the cheap. Some with an innocent, "Hey, I'm just building a little vacation cabin here, no biggie" sentiment, others with a more defiant, "Whadarya goin' to do about it, huh?" attitude. The firstcomers realized with sinking hearts that their once-idyllic, law-abiding retirement hideaway was facing ruination. Their only recourse, a Hail Mary, had been to demand that county authorities step in and rigorously enforce the building codes. Anything short of that and the place was toast.

And so it became toast.

Still a nice place to live, kinda sorta

Over time, the realm — a haphazard mix of approved residences, unsanctioned makeshift dwellings, unconnected mobile homes, trailers, RVs and tents — stabilized, after a fashion. It became perhaps not too unlike a cake that stopped rising in the oven, was removed, partially collapsed, then dried and solidified. Though essentially left precariously existing between two worlds, the Vista was effectively recycled as newcomers made like hermit crabs and moved into the rec land lot shells and houses abandoned by the previous inhabitants. Many came to consider the development a nice place to live despite its shortcomings and squirrelly history. Sure, it was a failed subdivision, but, hey, it was *our* failed subdivision.

Living in the Vista in its antediluvian days, before the sea of growers poured over the land and again altered its reason for being, was a bit like wearing a comfy, if disreputable-looking, old pair of sneakers that had yet to develop any worrisome holes in the soles.

Such indulgent regard for the place was *not* shared by most of the 80% of property holders as of 2010, over 1,200 absentee owners scattered across the nation. They were *not* enjoying the land. Some, possibly hoping for a miraculous turnaround, had clung to their title deeds for decades, gritting their teeth and doubling down year after year, shelling out for the upkeep of roads they never drove lest their lots be repossessed — as countless were over time. The common sentiment of such clueless owners of repo-ed lots must've been: "*When I invested in the place, I didn't realize I'd have to keep investing in it.*" Some, it seemed, couldn't get rid of their lots short of giving them away: "Take my land… *please.*"

Unkind thoughts

Indeed, many would eventually dump them in utter dismay, if not outright bitterness, taking the loss. They harbored distinctly unkind thoughts towards the once-promising place that turned out to be little more than a glorious half-baked fantasy that never panned out.

The churn rate of lot ownership changing hands, often due to foreclosure, lent a persistent sense of impermanence to the remote development gone astray. And created additional billing time for the salaried manager to process the reams of legal paperwork, thereby increasing association dues. And it generated quick commissions for profit-driven realtors who kept offering the embarrassment of beleaguered low-end lots as sleeper land deals to the uninformed, impulsive, desperate and expedient- or flip-minded. It often seemed they often didn't have to say a word; the generously sized, dirt-cheap lots with their sweeping mountain views and deep seclusion kept selling themselves.

Meanwhile, absentee parcel holders — like the hapless characters in *Waiting for Godot* — patiently stood by, expecting values to rise so they could *finally* lose the clunkers at a decent price or at least break even. Or, alternately, the place improved to the point that they might actually enjoy visiting, perhaps building a shelter for occasional retreats. Or, if they could afford it, maybe actually construct a code-approved home, sample Vista living for a while, then sell out for a nice profit once the place's charm began wearing thin. As it almost invariably did, a distinct disenchantment at some point taking hold, like having figured out how a magician performed his clever illusory trick.

"You'll love it here."

"Then why are you leaving?"

"Why? Er, well…"

CHAPTER 17

Beginnings re-examined: Ten-cent parcels with million-dollar views

The earliest campers in the newly formed shared wonderland savored it like fine wine. In spring, the realm delighted the senses with surprise splashes of lavender, purple, red and yellow wildflowers. Rich lichen moss on aging and dead junipers seemed magical, dazzling the eye with its near-phosphorescent chartreuse. After a drenching rain, the pungent scent of damp juniper and sagebrush was like perfume.

Abundant wildlife included deer, coyotes, jackrabbits and cottontails, birds of all kinds, ground squirrels and friendly chipmunks and less-friendly polecats, porcupines and rattle-snakes (the last now mostly, if not entirely, gone), a rare fox, mountain lion or other wildcat, at least one wild burro, and tiny, endangered kangaroo rats with impossibly long tails, hopping about at dusk.

The vacationers returned home refreshed, anticipating next year's visit to their new, yet untamed wilderness hideaway, imagining the improvements they'd make during future rendezvous with old friends and new acquaintances. They were filled with plans of carving out a happy retirement community sometime soon.

Seldom heard: a discouraging word

The vacationers would gather around the campfire at night. Coyotes yipped a storm in the distance, no doubt time-warping some back to days of the Old West and possibly inspiring spontaneous sing-alongs of "Home on the Range" and "Red River Valley." Hearing a distant train rumbling by higher up the mountain's foothills might've sparked an impromptu rendering of "I've Been Working on the Railroad."

In daytime, they enjoyed their potlucks and barbecues under the unfailing majesty of Mt. Shasta. The vantage point offered staggering views, highlighting its two massive, almost perennially snow- and glacier-covered peaks. In later years, photographer Kevin Lahey would race over from the city of Mt. Shasta to snap the spectacular, often surreal, lenticular, saucer-shaped clouds that sometimes flew off it. Or, on rare occasions, an impossibly huge one, filling much of the sky, hovered over it like a visiting mothership from Venus.

As evidenced by the writings in the association's semi-annual *Vistascope* newsletters, visitors shared in the euphoric waves of feel-goodness sweeping many parts of the planet during those rarefied purple-haze days (along with, of course, the gnarly uprisings, wars, race riots and protests).

... and the saucers flew by-y-y all night

Even if one was a hardline Vietnam War hawk and hostile to the emerging counterculture and its disturbing rejection of convention and shockingly liberated ways, spirits ran high — no doubt aided and abetted by their own mind-altering drug of choice, alcohol.

But the group buzz might've been further heightened by something more, something quite extraordinary: unknowingly receiving a cosmic buzz from the multiple UFOs spotted at the time darting about the mountain and making news head-lines. The embryonic community possibly gained a rarefied supercharge from curious, advanced beings visiting from other worlds, checking out the earthlings merrily enjoying the moun-tain's then super-sleepy side.

The dreamland's earliest imprints

To any susceptible to the subtle charms of the high desert woodlands, magnified under the mountain's spell, it was a nature lover's paradise. One that new parcel holders industri-ously worked at to make nicer. The light-duty cinder roads were kept immaculately groomed by the membership's workhorse road truck. Those with green thumbs planted flowers at select highway entrances. Others lifted the welcoming archway into place, maybe after a little dedication ceremony. Yet others estab-lished the de facto community well and holding tank.

It's said in metaphysical thinking that the imprint of the earliest inhabitants of a land creates a vibration that it then forever resonates with, no matter what might happen on it afterwards. If accepting this as maybe accurate... Prehistoric

American Indians hunted game here seasonally, often using Pluto Caves to trap bighorn sheep, but didn't settle because of the lack of water. Beyond them and the first isolated white settlers on the land — like Eli Barnum, by Sheep Rock, in the 1850s and, later, hunters and livestock grazers, including Gold Rush 49er Robert Martin, whose descendant sold the land — maybe the first lasting, indelible human imprint on the land had been made by none other than our modern-day refugees from smoggy L.A. (Who, you might say, left La-La Land to create a la-la land.)

If so, their earliest years of extended camping and, soon, settling, bestowed on the land an euphoric, industrious, decidedly conservative, somewhat topsy-turvy energy — a DNA signature the land still resonates with, even though often buried beneath the surface.

Apart from such possible influences on the subtle plane, whenever mindful visitors unwound and tuned into the land, they could sense its soft, almost otherworldly air. In spots beyond earshot of the highway wash, no jets droning overhead or freight trains rumbling in the distance, the land held such an ethereal quiet that one might've actually felt Earth breathing. Repeat visitors and residents alike, once adjusting to the all-enveloping silence, came to embrace it like a long-lost lover. Explorers of Pluto Caves, just beyond one of Vista's borders, might've experienced something of this etheric quality.

Serious downside

However, as mentioned, this dreamy atmosphere came with a downside. Tenuous new residents, wowed by the lightly wooded parcels bought for next to nothing, could get so caught up in spinning fantasies that they never did what needed to be done to get things squared away with the powers that be. And so they were never able to bring inspired brainstorms to fruition. Instead, they remained just so many pipe dreams inspired by the mountain's rarefied energies.

Over time, countless one-time owners came and went, happy bubbles burst after a few months or years on the land, either ignoring or being ignorant of the sundry mundane regulatory realities fitfully enforced by the county government. Ordinances that would have owners jump through all kinds of hoops before getting the green light to build to steep and pricey standards. And then, out of the blue, a reality check would shock them awake like a bucket of ice water over the head.

It was a predictable pattern. The serene, enchanted land, for sale cheap, kept drawing newbies stoked over the remote parcels' possibilities. It was like a 'Star Trek' TV episode in which the intrepid space explorers beam down to a strange new planet that at first appears to be some wondrous paradise. Then, inevitably, a menace pops up, and they're lucky to get away alive.

A fine place, by George: Further speculations on why things went so far south

Developer George Collins seemed no less smitten by the land's charms than the earlycomers he and his associates sold the lots to. Besides a fellow vacationer, he was a superglue holding the place together, serving as father, midwife, cheerleader, first board president and daddy moneybags all rolled into one. He pitched in with funds and resources to help the place along at every turn. "… I consider myself privileged to be a neighbor to each and every one of you," he wrote in an early newsletter with obvious feeling. He went on to wax poetic about how the place was "… our home away from home, our frontier, our Shangri-la … there should be a constant flurry of barbecue parties, coffee klatches and just informal get-togethers all through the year."

But alas, he'd begun what was destined to become a stupendous developmental misfire — a stalled-out, bare-bones recreational subdivision lacking any more ambitious, well-defined plans at the start and, soon after it became a residential community, attracting those without the will or wherewithal to continue developing the place to accepted standards. The raw land, super-affordable and enjoyable for primitive campouts, as a would-be living community caused headaches and heartbreak for all, especially the less-affluent would-be residents who, of necessity, became "outlaw" dwellers.

That said, he was far from being your stereotypical, slick, disinterested land developer who took the money and ran. He nurtured the place along at every step, wanting to see it flourish — at least as a collectively owned, simple camp resort — maybe more, so long as it was understood he wasn't on the hook for building up further infrastructure. Any interested parties would have to bear that financial burden themselves.

'Let George do it'

He was so central to the place's early years that other property owners must have grown accustomed to leaving everything in his capable hands. Perhaps on one level they'd become like land tenants, relying on their kind overlord to do whatever needed to be done: "Let George do it."

In essence, he was the place's benevolent master, doing all the heavy lifting and sparing others the bother. (In so doing, he undoubtedly built up the wilderness turn-key wilderness condo feel to the place: Management took care of *every*thing.) He was acknowledged as the leading man by willing and grateful subjects for as long as he stayed in the picture. Consequently, few probably ever felt motivated or empowered to launch independent efforts to grow the place according to their own lights. Until people actually started building and moving onto their parcels, it remained *his* baby.

At some point, though, he'd step down, for reasons unclear. No doubt it was somehow connected to the first residents-to-be gaining serious, invested interest in the place's future as a living community and, finally, empowering themselves to go for it. Perhaps they felt that if he weren't also going to build a home and reside here like them, he'd no longer fit into the picture.

In any event, vacationers and new residents would be forced to scramble once their one-time master organizer bowed out. Left to their own devices, they'd face a steep learning curve, assuming responsibilities and grappling with sundry matters, some of which they probably never even knew existed.

It was likely at this point that the good ship Vista first began to seriously founder. Sure, it'd probably had its problems before — bothersome leaks that required bailing efforts to stay shipshape. But Collins, seasoned subdivision developer, had seemed to know — until the electrification brouhaha went down, anyway, unraveling the early, tenuously unified efforts — how to deal with and resolve whatever problems might crop up. Now, property owners, forsaken by their captain, would be left to get their bearings and steer a course under their own steam, while also stepping up bailing efforts to avoid getting thoroughly swamped.

Alas, no critical mass

Apparently, enough original lot holders had been jazzed by the idea of building a retirement community, plus by next-door Lake Shastina taking off, that Collins's hopes had risen after having cautiously played it by ear at first. "If enough of you want to build a residential community, I'm your man to help you get it done (on your dime, of course)" might've essentially been his attitude. But he'd lost his grip on the place once the first few dozen landowners began settling in and future power extension costs almost certainly went through the roof.

More knowledgeable association members must've realized that the widely scattered residential base might likely never reach the saturation level needed to ensure that future residents would continue meeting health and building code require-ments. Consequently, the development, lacking an effective enforcement arm, would always be super vulnerable to lot holders intent on moving in on the cheap.

Plus, water was often so deep and power so pricey — and soured speculators so unwilling to sink another penny in the place by special assessment for any reason — that its chances of remaining a respectable, law-abiding enclave might have appeared slim to none.

It was soon evident, after the brief burst of settlement efforts, that only a tiny number had been keen to move onto the land. It must've seemed to others that they'd be throwing good money after bad to invest in building homes in what was already showing early signs of being a stalled-out development. It was a place that might, very likely, never amount to being more than a sparsely settled, perpetually challenged, would-be exclusive community. One with its few dwellings spaced out amid a sea of empty, now-obsolete camping lots. One too far in the sticks to attract any beyond a few well-heeled retirees, and, soon, their antithesis, the younger, would-be back-to-the-landers living on a shoestring, who would in due course upend the place's respectable, convention-locked, retiring ambiance.

Builders and would-be builders became increasingly frustrated and testy over the lack of easy water, especially on realizing that people 15 miles away could hit good water at 75 feet or less. Vistan settlers routinely had to drill at least four times that depth, costing a small fortune, and then, assuming they even hit, might have to deal with suspended arsenic and iron.

Lost heart

It's said that it's easy to come and go but hard to stay. Lot owners who first moved onto the land after years of only visiting knew they'd have to carry on under their own steam — each supplying their own water, power and septic at great effort, time and expense. Collins's role and influence, once paramount, had shrunk to nothing beyond an honorary position as people, perforce, began forging ahead on their own.

Likely feeling hurt after all he'd done for the place, sensing the uneasy divisions splitting the ranks and an eroded regard for him once he lost his firm grip in the power-and-light melt-down, he might've at last said the hell with it… and his blessing turned into something less kind. At the very least, he might've copped a bittersweet, newly detached attitude of, *Well, I wish you all the best of luck; I'm outta here.* He had more than fulfilled his legal obligations and wanted to wash his hands of further involvement with the place he'd birthed and nurtured and had held such high (if perhaps unrealistic) hopes for.

And so, it's possible that lot holders' fading happy vision of spending their golden years in Mt. Shasta Vista's peaceful seclusion began its long, sorrowful slide into oblivion even as the first homes were being built. Without their one-time champion cheering them on and uniting them, constructing their future homes might have left a hollow-victory feeling, a gnawing sense of guilt for having perhaps told him where to get off.

Something had turned the wine into vinegar. Something — or series of somethings — occurred to change the entire trajectory of the one-time Shangri-la from incipient idyllic rural retirement community — sweet hideaway, rich with promise — into a busted dream and budding nightmare.

CHAPTER 18

A hundred times better deal?

Vista's raw parcels on a per-acre basis were at once 10 times cheaper and 10 times bigger than those of the almost next-door exurb of Lake Shastina. That meant that for any land shopper like me, not unduly concerned about its unabashed lack of infrastructure (or preferring it), its relative remoteness, or its quirky, haywire history, the Vista represented a deal 100 times better.

But to others, those of the more conventional bent, of the home-is-an-investment-first-and-foremost mindset, and hooked on city amenities, the lots held precious little value. Not since their reason for being had gotten so hopelessly hamstrung, stuck between serving as basic camping retreats and places too pricey and challenging to build conventional homes on. As the number of non-code dwellings increased, the place's air of well-bred gentility degenerated, with a few nicer homes here and there to remind others how ambitious and hopeful the place once was.

Vista had at first attracted as much of a financially secure crowd as the second-home buyers in Lake Shastina, whom developers courted with full-on infrastructure, an artificial lake and, the clincher for some, an 18-hole championship golf course *plus* a nine-hole Scottish links course. But Vista's population base shifted radically once enough code ignorers moved in, its brief allure as an upscale-rustic hamlet vanishing in an instant. It became a rural ghetto to conventional thinking, scorned as a dead-in-the-water development. On the practical level, it was deemed as little more than an unfortunate wasteland (if a still somewhat charming one).

Comparing the two developments, situated so closely together, became like comparing apples and oranges. One was a full-fledged standard community, the other was futilely scrambling to try to return to one while its less solvent or convention-minded dwellers were A-okay with it just the way it was, thank you.

Lookin' for a sign amid the maze of roads

One thing the Vista had long kept on top of was road signs, even if its initial four-foot-tall, wooden 4 x 4 ones proved undersized and short-lived.

Road signs were crucial inside the endless 66-mile labyrinth. Even longtime residents like me sometimes got lost if we ventured off our habitual routes. One moonless night, I was driving about in another section and suddenly realized I had no idea where I was. Completely disoriented, I drove on for what felt like forever before reaching an intersection. There, spotting a stenciled signpost, I climbed out and hopefully shone my flashlight on it, expecting to regain my bearings with the help of my trusty tiny road map and strong reading glasses. But the painted lettering had faded to illegibility, done in by the elements; I was still lost in a place I'd called home for decades.

The second-generation signs were equally modest, four-foot-high painted-steel affairs that soon rusted. Delinquents would steal or tip them, as well as the current third-generation, eight-foot-tall rustproof reflective-green metal signs, their poles set in concrete. Perhaps they felt the latter's slick, citified appearance clashed with the place's primitive ambiance. Or they may have wanted to make it harder for anyone to find their place, should they not *want* to be found, leaving those unfamiliar with the roads so disoriented that they'd want to switch gears to escape the bewildering maze.

A new version of the current third-generation signs has proved interesting. The board either started ordering them from a new source or the old one had cheapened their product. In any event, the road lettering that was formerly durably baked on was now apparently only a transparency. It looked fine at first. Then, after a few summers went by, the sun beating down on the decals, the lettering turned all but invisible. The current profusion of blank road signs about the place is maybe apropos in a way: They seemed to say "You're here, but if you don't know where here is, we're not going to help you."

The great robin invasion

Robins often find slim pickings during winter and early spring and resort to eating juniper berries to get by. There have been several documented reports — in Portland, OR, Georgia, Texas and Rhode Island — of the birds becoming inebriated after scarfing the berries, as their natural sugars ferment into alcohol when the returning warm sun hits them. The moister the weather, the higher the fruit production. We must've had a very wet winter one year (I've forgotten which year, I think sometime in the 1990s). Plus we must've had a particularly abundant crop of ripe berries, for the land was about to experience something quite extraordinary.

What was perhaps the largest gathering of robins ever to gorge on juniper berries in recent U.S. history happened right here. Being smack dab in the middle of an extensive spread of Western Junipers, and the warmth of spring coming here sooner than many places for being in a high-desert banana belt, hastening early berry ripening, the ravenous robins' overmind must've telepathically spread the word to every member on the West Coast: Plentiful eats and a wild time to be had if you fly west at Mt. Shasta.

Doing the math floored me: 1,641 Vista lots, each having, conservatively, 50 trees — half of them female, or fruit-producing trees — and each bearing tree with thousands of berries (sometimes half ripe, half green, as the same tree's fruit can have a staggered two-year maturing cycle). With each bearing tree attracting, say, 25 birds (some mature trees, which can produce lots more berries, were easily laden with over 50 birds)… that's 1,641 lots x 25 fruit-producing trees per lot x 25 birds working each tree = 1,025,625 robins.

Over a million birds. All feasting away within the Vista boundaries alone that spring, and maybe half again as many in the surrounding wooded areas. It surely lured every single robin within migrating distance. Since robins can seasonally fly thousands of miles, up to 250 miles a day if *really* motivated (as no doubt they were), every robin within a 1,000-mile radius must have made a beeline for the trees.

One had to see it to believe it. Trees everywhere were alive with the noisy, madly gobbling birds, feasting away like it was some avian 1,000-year celebration and getting royally drunk in the process. It drove more than a few residents nuts. The birds made such a loud clatter on their mobile homes' metal roofs and tweeted such a deafening storm in the trees that they fired guns to scare them away; this provided only a few minutes' respite before they returned in renewed frenzy. They often got disoriented and lost coordination from the alcohol; one neighbor told me he saw a bird that was so schnock-ered, it toppled from its perch and fell to the ground, dead drunk.

Part of me felt like reporting the extraordinary event to the media or the Audubon Society; I wish I had now. It was such an incredible event, hard to believe if you hadn't witnessed it yourself. But, living in Vista's sleepy mañana land, inertia prevailed. And so the phenomenal occurrence — a week-long bacchanalia of myriad, ravenous, noisy robins, soon besotted, adorning Mt. Shasta Vista's junipers in an overwhelming pres-ence — likely came and went unreported, undocumented and unnoticed beyond Vista's own astonished residents.

Sheer number of phantom
residents haunted the place

Countless lot holders had snapped up the cheap parcels out of pure speculation — plus maybe, for some, to gain bragging rights for owning a piece of the Golden State and relishing the novelty of being a landholder. They hoped that eventual improvements, such as centralized water and extensive power lines, or at least everyone building to code and supplying their own water and power, would someday boost property values.

Being the first kid on the block in the wider region's advent of rural subdivisions, the Vista might've served in effect as a de facto test run for the other California realtors who'd soon launch their own rural developments. They may have taken note and fine-tuned their projects accordingly, providing more infrastructure and a formal plan for residential growth. Vista's fast-selling lots proved there was indeed a market (if maybe only for affordable rec lots at first). Meanwhile, the Vista was held back and incapacitated by its initial low ambition, despite approved homes popping up here and there.

One couldn't resist the bargain price. Perhaps the saying "What we obtain too cheaply, we esteem too lightly" proved true in Vista's case. Over the years, properties traded hands like so many baseball cards at recess. If each parcel on average changed ownership three times over its 50 years up to 2015 (probably an underestimate), the place experienced a rotation of ownership among some 5,000 parties located throughout the nation. If you added two other family members per parcel getting involved, the total rose to *15,000* people, each with varying degrees of vested interest in the place.

Fifteen thousand individuals — the overwhelming number absentee owners — were bound to keep the beleaguered outlands feeling more than a little sketchy around the edges.

It might have struck some that the place had always seemed to be more of an abstract commercial aggregate of raw-land commodities, to be speculated on like so many soybean futures, rather than any actual physical development. Massive speculation eclipsed appreciation for any practical value the parcels might have.

Treacherous psychic undertow and a Mount Everest of inertia

After the retiree flock largely faded away and a diverse population, some short-term, came to dominate, civic interest became almost nil. Latter-day, socially-minded newcomers who plugged in and got involved quickly became aware of the realm's massive psychic undertow and its Mt. Everest of inertia. Such forces — reinforced by the board, the only organized group the place had other than its volunteer fire department and auxiliary fundraiser — could dampen enthusiasm for getting involved in record time. It fostered a sense of futility about ever trying to fix *anything*. Treading water seemed the only thing one could do; anything more appeared a fool's errand.

The place was like a disastrous big-budget movie misfire where everything went wrong after a promising start, the creative vision never realized.

First-involved newcomers became disappointed and gave up or hastily dialed back any errant urges to get involved. The few undeterred, more thick-skinned and unwavering could appear as so many Don Quixotes tilting at windmills.

Meanwhile, the expansive place remained relatively bereft of residents, maybe 250 at most. That's roughly 35 people per square mile (compared to over 18,000 in San Francisco or 27,000 in New York City). Until 2015's dramatic land-use changes and population explosion, absentee lot owners still outnumbered residents roughly seven to one.

Fraught with paradox

The first wave of settlers was flush with cash and jazzed at the prospect of becoming modern-day pioneers and forging their own law-abiding, sparsely settled, semi-tamed wilderness community. Some, again, must have nurtured hopes that the place would grow as other retirees, plus maybe decent working folks willing to accept and acquiesce to their urbane ways of running things, joined the venerable oldsters.

But others were possibly less altruistic and expansion-minded and perhaps more than a smidgen drunk with the power born of sudden liquid wealth and having made such a momentously bold move. They became uber-territorial over their former camp land and hoped to metamorphose it into serving as essentially their own residential community, wanting everything to be just so. With the soaring home values they'd cashed out on and being ready to downsize, they could easily afford to build fully compliant if more modest homes in Siskiyou County, with its lower cost of living, and still have a good chunk of change left over; they were sitting pretty.

It would become a place where they, as the well-off founders, had established a comfortable rural standard of living that any others, if likewise financially secure and liking what they did (and weren't put off by their pronounced urbane So-Cal air), would gladly conform to. Nobody would dare try to move in on the cheap amid their respectable, law-abiding hideaway, not if they knew what was good for them.

It might be hard for some to appreciate, in our extreme times, how such health and building codes could have ever been so rigorously enforced in such a remote land. But they were... or tried to be. And the first wave of owner builders, staunch upright citizens that they were, having jumped through every single blasted hoop and never thinking not to, fully expected anyone else wanting to live here to do the same blessed thing. It was simply the price one paid to gain entry to the special sanctuary; one *earned* the right to live here. Try sneaking in and avoiding the steep admission price, and it was "throw the bum out."

The way they went bonkers once instant homesteaders became a force to be reckoned with, some might've concluded that the situation smacked of bitter irony. After all, the place had started out by championing primitive campgrounds. But then, when people began settling, they grew so territorial that they became wary of anyone still using the lots for camping. The place had turned 180 degrees. Residents became so leery of campers (except perhaps ones in fancy RVs) that they'd zealously tracked their remaining allowable camping days before they could throw them under the bus in righteous anger by reporting the miscreants to proper authorities.

The place had began as a collection of casual, do-your-own-thing recreational lots, then tried transforming into a standard residential community only to get bogged down between the two worlds. Its reason for being became muddier than the Mississippi in late spring, and so would end up supporting neither.

CHAPTER 19

Power to the people
(some, anyhow)

In the early seventies, the handful of property owners intent on building their retirement homes needed electricity, and power lines were nowhere to be found. Others may have hoped to have electricity made available for camp visits in their appliance-loaded trailers and RVs. But if so, perhaps unbeknownst to them, authorities and the power company probably wouldn't have allowed temporary hook-ups short of restructuring the entire grounds into one humongous trailer park. Maybe they'd hoped extending power would at least expedite the creation of a facility where campers could do loads of laundry, shower, use a pay phone, dump RV holding tanks, maybe recharge a dead battery, without having to drive clear to town.

But others, almost certainly the overwhelming majority, in donating to the power-and-light fund had likely only wanted to goose lot values and sellability by adding such basic infrastructure. They hoped to make the lots more attractive to those maybe toying with the idea of building, if only a modest vacation cabin.

Enough had seemed interested in making the go juice available — but not enough to vote for a mandatory assessment to fund wiring the whole place. So they made it a volunteer assessment, hoping to spread the otherwise prohibitive cost of extending power lines to the remote parcels of whoever was serious about building.

Possibly, Collins had the idea of adding electricity in mind all along, or did once he saw nearby Lake Shastina taking off. Were there enough owners interested in further developing the place, or were they more content to let it remain the way it was, a de facto seasonal primitive camp resort and modest sleeper investment.

If the former proved true, it wasn't an option but a given that the ubiquitous energy elixir so much of humanity was unabashedly hooked on needed to be brought in posthaste. If the latter were the case, bringing in power, while *maybe* goosing property values, would of course sound the death knell for the place's halcyon days of primitive camping.

As usual, Mt. Shasta's dream factory was at work. Ambition appeared poised to make a quantum leap as certain property owners, led by Collins, envisioned extending electrical lines to every last lot. Why not? The power company — again, possibly on the strength of developer Collins's assurances he'd work to get everyone on board — reportedly made a tentative commitment to extend power lines throughout, pending sufficient funding by the association. Anything short of a mandatory assessment, of course, and they'd only wire as much as the limited fund allowed.

Turning point

The backwoods camp realm was possibly on the verge of transforming, if only in a haphazard, scrambling to catch up, slapdash sort of way. If enough went along, it could be on its way to segueing into an actual bona fide community of sorts. It would have met one of a place's three vital infrastructure needs, leaving water supply and hygienic waste disposal yet to be reckoned with. Any lot owners wanting to settle would themselves continue being responsible for generating these individually for the foreseeable future.

But not enough went along. While three in four, or some 1,200 parcel holders, chipped in — either fired up over the prospect of building or thinking adding power would boost parcel values — a quarter of the membership flat-out refused. Some 400 lot owners wouldn't contribute, despite Collins' pleaful pitch in the *Vistascope* newsletter that started, "I know each of you bought lots out in the middle of nowhere so that you could do with whatever you damn well please with it, but…", going on to try convincing the hold-outs to reconsider.

To no avail.

It seemed that many who actually *visited* their parcels and savored the place's serenity had been hunky dory with the primitive parcels just the way they were, thank you. They relished roughing it on their own bit of wilderness and knew adding unsightly power and phone lines, with their intrusive, dead-tree, creosote-soaked poles and high-strung, EMF-emitting wires, would ruin things faster than you could say "power bill." They'd mar the natural realm's semi-pristine charm that they'd bought the inexpensive, primitive parcels for: simple camp vacations. They had never intended to do anything with them beyond, at most, roughing in a driveway, making a tent or trailer clearing, and building a stone campfire ring; maybe, if really ambitious, building an outhouse with crescent moon on the door.

Getting away from it all

The whole idea of the place, as they saw it, was to serve as a getaway from the complexities of modern life — including electrical dependency and telephones (this was, of course, decades before the advent of cell phones and solar power). Get back to basics, not drag the buggers in. They wanted to push the reset button and recharge within the still semi-wild place. Those leaning this way may have thought the place so remote that further development appeared unlikely. They hoped their parcels would continue to serve as private, primitive refuges — not only for themselves, but for family and friends or anyone they might decide to sell them to.

Even though the lots *were* rezoned for single-resident occupancy, providing a potential avenue for building out a standard living community, it must've appeared to many who declined to chip in that speculation fever was out of control; people seemed to be betting unrealistically on robust growth, like in Lake Shastina.

Too late, the former realized there weren't enough others interested in settling, thereby effectively indeed leaving some 98% of the parcels empty, no longer suitable for full-on camping retreats and too pricey to build on. They became virtually unusable beyond maybe getting firewood from or, for various new agers, harvesting the plentiful mountain sagebrush stems to wrap into purification smudge sticks.

Sea of disinterested speculators

Some who refused to chip in were themselves likely disinterested investors and speculators. They'd perhaps already soured on the place they had somehow managed to get themselves tangled up in against their better judgment. Property values were failing to increase; their anticipated easy money making proved to be a cruel mirage.

The cynically inclined might have jumped to the conclusion that a select few parcel owners, primed to make the grand leap and build new residences, had craftily persuaded over 1,000 others to contribute to the power fund just to minimize their own outlays.

In any case, various lot holders were, quite understandably, loath to sink another blessed cent in the place. Some possibly reasoned that getting power to every lot by itself wouldn't appreciably increase the parcels' market values, due to the remaining iffy water situation and at times problematic waste-disposal issue. Possible further thinking: Not enough would ever want to live out in the middle of nowhere, so far from accustomed city conveniences and having to wrestle with providing their own infrastructure, beyond a few kooky retirees who, it seemed, wanted to leave the whole bloomin' world behind. More rational-thinking owners might not have blamed them a bit, some perhaps even envying and admiring their boldness. Still, they might have been furious over the almost certain line-extension cost increase from Pacific Power.

Sorry, out of luck, schmuck; lights out

The power-and-light fund had been a flash in the pan: first come, first served, good 'til gone. It was gone fast. A couple of dozen parcel owners went for it — psyched at the idea of living in such splendid seclusion. Or of building structures for others to get enthused about after they enjoyed them until the novelty of Vista living wore off, and they sold them to others likewise smitten by the place. The power company, realizing the association wouldn't approve mandatory assessments to cover the cost of stringing the whole place, backed out of its tenuous commitment to a complete wiring campaign. They'd been discouraged, anyhow, by the frequent drill-bit-shattering lava-rock strata their crews encountered that required expensive part replacements. (A similar problem was no doubt experienced by various owners trying to excavate workable conventional septic systems on rocky or sloping parcels.)

But before the tide turned and the perhaps overly ambitious plan fell through, Pacific Power, showing its initial good-faith commitment, had installed and wired towering street lamps at all five highway entrances. They would perhaps still be shining away at night today but for the beacons (which gave off an eerie, cold, bluish-white glow) continually being shot out by rowdy locals. Their tribe was still fulminating over the subdivision's very existence. They must have taken especially keen delight in being able to sabotage the contemptible place without even having to leave the blacktop. After a few rounds of such target practice and the power company's dutiful repairs, the latter finally gave up and removed the lights. The five highway entrances once again were swallowed by darkness after nightfall.

This malicious mischief shows, perhaps better than anything, how deeply locals' bitterness ran towards the upstart development with the gall to have taken over *their* land: They'd undoubtedly cast one mighty hex over it. Their message, loud and clear: "It's lights out for you guys; take it back to Long Beach."

The troubled outlands' hapless parcel owners — forever at odds with one another over future land use, under relentless attack by intolerant locals and now likely feeling screwed by the power company — were left twisting in the wind.

CHAPTER 20

Short-lived cooperative efforts

Although no more than about 6% of the 1,641 parcels ever got connected to the power grid, some who contributed to the fund undoubtedly had at least tentative plans to maybe build in the future. They were likely discouraged by the fund's rapid depletion — and furious at the power company, if it indeed raised prices so prohibitively that affordable line extensions became a thing of the past. They sold their lots (or tried to), feeling dismayed and disappointed, if not spitting-nails mad: Their dream hideaway became too costly to build on.

Some of the less informed who'd chipped in and kept their lots and thought to build sometime down the road, undoubtedly lost it on realizing they'd been left out in the cold. When they were ready to construct, the power company probably quoted them a shocking five-digit figure that could've caused heart failure. The more cynical and uninformed might've concluded that the company had reneged on its earlier commitment through some underhanded bait-and-switch.

The firstcomers had realized that the fund would cover line-extension costs for only a limited number of lot owners. (By 2024, extension costs were over $53,000 a mile, or about $10 a foot.) Being new-fledged retirees who had both the means and the desire to re-settle, they'd moved fast, maybe faster than they wanted to if having gotten some inside skinny on soon-to-soar extension rates, but extra motivation to go for it while the getting was good. In any event, the limited-fund situation had definitely favored the quick and the bold.

The vicious circle kept going round and round

The way the place moved from one crisis to another was amusing, seen from the perspective of the grand, ongoing tragi-comic human drama, which one could either cry about, laugh at, or both by turn.

The earliest campers became the bad guys to the locals who resented their land takeover. Then those who ruined the place for camping by building homes and got overly territorial became the devils to the rest of the lot owners who'd taken the land from the locals. Then those who ignored building codes — suspected of growing pot whether they were or not — became the miscreants to the code-legal residents who'd ruined the place for camping for those who'd taken the land from the locals. Then unlicensed pot growers became the scoundrels to the code-legal residents who'd ruined the place for camping for the other lot owners who'd taken the land from the locals.

Then the residents who stayed, suspected if *not* growing pot for having no skin in the game, became the villains to the growers who…

The vicious circle just kept going round and round. (And this, of course, didn't even include the pioneer white settlers who'd crowded away the land's use by seasonally visiting American Indians.)

Place failed to catch the solar-electric wave

Mt. Shasta Vista missed a sure bet by not going solar. Between the place's enviable banana-belt microclimate, advancing solar technology and plummeting costs, it was the ideal solution for supplying go juice to the grid-challenged area. With its high-desert location, it could be so sunshiny on some March days that one might be relaxing and enjoying soaking in the rays, while in Weed, 15 miles away, hunched-over snow shovelers still only dreamed of spring.

The first believed solar-electric system in Shasta Vista was installed in the 1970s by code-compliant resident Brian Green, a late co-founder of *Homepower* magazine, which later became the premier global resource guide for creating do-it-yourself alternative-energy off-grid systems. This was, of course, decades before mainstream industry ever got involved after realizing solar electricity was the wave of the future.

In 1989, I became one of only two known Vista residents (the other being board president Pam Simpson, who bought Brian Green's place from his widow), to rely exclusively on solar electricity. In my case, it was sunshine or bust: no backup generator.

A 1992 *HomePower* article on my tiny 120-watt system was featured in issue #30 as an example of a modest setup. (With my spare lifestyle, after 36 years, my setup would only grow to 300 watts; a typical solar home nowadays is between 5 and ten kilowatts, or over 15 to 30 times larger.) The editors wanted to show that one didn't have to spend a fortune to create an off-grid system *if* content to have only the most basic electrical amenities covered, then using alternative sources for the rest, such as a propane for refrigeration, cooking and hot water, *lots* of south-facing windows and an efficient wood stove for heating. (Although *Homepower* ceased publication in November 2018, its entire archives are available to download for free with a simple sign-up at homepower.com.)

In startling contrast to Mt. Shasta Vista, the McCloud region's Shasta Forest development, even further from the grid, fully embraced solar as the most affordable — not to mention environmentally friendly — solution for powering its many sometimes quite substantial residences. (The Vista might've as well in time, had it remained code-compliant.)

Well, well

Developer Collins and the early owner volunteers established the informal, in effect community well and constructed a giant holding tank, sporting an enormous overhead valve, which all Vista lot holders were welcome to tap for free, filling the community water truck, until their own wells were in. A garden spigot was provided to fill containers for camping visits. When the truck was later switched to fire use only, those with prohibitively deep water tables — mostly in Section 23, where 700-foot or deeper wells were required — still found it challenging to get working wells in. My neighbor, Bill Waterson, had three costly drilling misses, ironic, given his name. (Much later, an older Hmong neighbor, Kee, wouldn't hit even after drilling *800* feet.) Affected parties formed Property Owners Without Water (POWW), an apt acronym, given the place's tense social climate, and got another water truck together.

Closing the unofficial quasi-community watering hole

In 1980, it came to light at the county health department, following stricter California water-use laws, that the unofficial, never-sanctioned community well was illegal. And the water truck was uncertified to deliver potable water and lacked an ostensibly required certified delivery person. Then-department head Dr. Bayuk capped the membership of the 25 resident owners with an iron fist. He told us at a specially called meeting held at the McLarty Road home of then-board president and POWW member, John Shelton, that since he held discretionary powers to grant a code variance, he'd let current POWW members — but *only* POWW members — continue hauling from the well.

This consideration was given in light of numerous respectable individuals having sold their former homes and built in the Vista on the strength of realtors' assurances that there was a community well, so one didn't need to bring in a well before building. It seems the health department took pity on them (or maybe wanted to avoid a lawsuit against the county if they tried to shut down the long-established well outright). The building department, working in tandem with health, honored the variance, issuing permits to any well-less parcel holders who were POWW members, then expecting them to fully comply with all other building requirements.

He told us that all other lot holders would now have to drill an approved well before they could apply for a building permit. He envisioned the POWW memberships — nontransferable to anyone they might sell their places to — fading away over time as lot holders either installed wells, died, or sold properties to others, who'd then be expected to drill an approved well before moving in.

Honor system

We were on the honor system. Inertia, ridiculously strong in the Vista, reigned supreme. And a way of living had long been established. Some who were otherwise compliant, rather than spring for a well, resigned themselves to continuing to haul water as the price one paid for living here affordably. And so the audaciously non-compliant dwellers, hunkering down hopefully below the radar of snoopy neighbors and the powers that be, kept filling up at the well as usual. Residents were keen on the idea of avoiding the high expense (assuming they could afford it) of a drilling effort that might not even reach water, or good water, or sufficient water — plus the prohibitive cost of extending electrical lines to power the well pump and eventual dwelling.

As a result, although POWW membership's water-hauling rights were technically nontransferable, the regulation was seldom, if ever, enforced. It became yet another of man's myriad rules and policies ignored as if it didn't exist.

Decades later, there were still over half a dozen otherwise code-legal homes in one section alone for which water hauling rights had technically been voided ages ago through property transfers. Yet current owners were still merrily schlepping in loads of water. The county apparently didn't feel the need to mess with homes once they'd passed final inspection; the code enforcers' job was done as far as they were concerned. Never told otherwise, new homeowners assumed that water-hauling rights *were* transferable.

This gave prospective residents the impression that one needn't bring in a well before applying for a building permit. It seemed you could build first, then, sometime down the road, try for a well at your own convenience — or not, your choice. This misunderstanding was destined to further baffle many future would-be residents (as well as newer health department workers): "Lots of homes don't have wells, but they got building permits; why can't I?"

While Dr. Bayuk had cautioned Vista board members against allowing anyone to use the well beyond POWW's now-closed membership, efforts to restrict access were, of course, ineffective. Padlocks kept getting cut with bolt cutters by water-jonesin' scofflaws, and the idea of fencing off access was likely seen as more work and expense than anyone wanted to mess with. Obviously, no one wanted to volunteer for guard duty.

Over time, the ever-changing board members apparently either lost track of the county's well-use stipulation or overlooked it, along with the county. Perhaps some felt that the well symbolized the one thing that property owners had worked on together to forge an actual community. Amid the sorrowful confusion and contention that befell the place over time, the venerable well and its giant holding tank had served as a visible reminder of its once-promising prospects from a time when landholders actually worked together to improve the place.

'Hey, it comes with the property... doesn't it?'

Fast-forward decades, and the well use situation was still out of control. Residents living on the cheap, never intending to drill, kept openly tapping it. One short-term resident living in a shack on Placone Road would make daily hot-summer water runs for his teeming menagerie of thirsty livestock in an ancient Cadillac, back seat removed and crammed full, along with the trunk, with lidded five-gallon buckets and Jerry cans.

Some, perhaps a bit *too* bohemian, reportedly copped showers there by attaching a hose and spray nozzle to the spigot. Risking being seen showering naked in full view of the then-infrequent traffic along a road 60 feet away must've felt worth it for the chance to luxuriate in a fast cool-down and rehydration on a scorching hot day. As mentioned, some free spirit residents often went about nude or semi-nude (albeit mainly on their own remote properties) in nice weather, so such public showering may not have seemed that outre and shocking. The Vista was such a primitive, rarefied spot with a magical climate that, in another time and circumstance (and with more water), it might've made a dandy naturist resort.

Finally, board members, led by then-president George Gosting, feared being fined by the state or sued by the membership for permitting continued well use. Well-owning residents fumed over how their annual dues were being used to replace the pump and cover its monthly power bills; they felt they were essentially not only enabling but *subsidizing* code noncompliance. The board came up with a solution: Get rid of the bugger. They quickly sold it outright, with no public discussion or prior notice. Done deal, end of story. Except for the unbridled fury of countless well-less, mostly non-compliant residents, suddenly left high and dry.

And they got sued anyhow, by an irate interracial couple in Section 23, Alex and Debbie Blume, who briefly lived in an otherwise code-approved but well-less modular dwelling on Stewart Road, first owned by the Miller family, who'd been longtime POWW members. The suit pursued far-fetched racketeering charges. They'd likely relied on the erroneous assumption that their home had legal water-hauling rights from the well, so the association couldn't sell the well and leave people who depended on it in the lurch. Alas, they lost the case, and the lawyer, for his trouble, got their practically *new*, convertible Cadillac signed over as part payment.

'It's all a big scam, I tell ya'

Between earlier, fitfully enforced legal-residency codes and the demise of the longtime de facto community well, it must've seemed to non-compliant dwellers, told to get a well or else, that a draconian building moratorium had been clamped on the place. Of course, it was all standard procedure to gain legal residency anywhere in California. But our place had always felt exceptional for having difficult water and being in such remote hinterlands — and perhaps most of all for being under Mt. Shasta's spell and its sometimes almost otherworldly energy.

The Vista was a dreamland, pure and simple. Somehow, it felt beyond the pale of the mundane world and all its nitpicky rules and regulations. It was a realm unto itself, operating on its own frequency, penciling in rules as current residents saw fit, and even then they were only suggestions.

As a result, various land-hungry buyers on a tight budget, lured by the bargain lands and failing to exercise due diligence, felt majorly scammed when at some point they got hassled by irate code-legal residents and the county and told they couldn't stay on their properties more than 30 days a year before first doing this, that, and the other thing. They'd accuse the association board, management and realtors of being in cahoots somehow, each passing the buck, no one being accountable. To a suspicious mind, not always able or willing to understand and deal with the frequently unreasonable ways of the world, it might've indeed seemed as though they were all slyly working together, churning out problematic marginal properties for quick gain while keeping rigid control over everything.

It was obvious, in any event, that self-interested forces *were* exploiting people's desire to own their own land, all too aware that many couldn't begin to meet the legal residency requirements short of winning a lottery or some rich old aunt dying. But hey, it was always buyer beware.

Unending cycle

The unending cycle, as the uninformed parcel holders saw it: A lot was sold after the realtor maybe downplayed the legal snags of residing on it as-is, offering a wink as if to say the rules often went unenforced; the purchaser, disillusioned once getting routed by angry legal residents, board members and county authorities, quit paying annual POA assessment in protest; in time the lot was foreclosed on, the Association repossessed it, and it was re-listed, realtors waiting for next sucker to come along.

In later times, many buyers knew the score but didn't care. In a new era with a radically different social climate and sketchier building-code enforcement, they were game to join Vista's growing population of non-compliant and *what's-it-to-you?* dwellers. Again, they'd been emboldened after the county axed its residential-code enforcer position during the critical five-year period following the Great Recession of 2008-09. By the time the position was finally reinstated, it lacked the will to resume enforcing legal residency requirements — at least in the Vista. Clearly, by then, the county viewed the place as only a greater mess, one it seemed best to continue ignoring.

I attended the county board of supervisors' public meeting at which the enforcement position was finally re-funded. I was struck by their apparent reluctance to act and by how detached they appeared from the significance of the regulatory role for taxpaying residents who, not unreasonably, expected to enjoy peace of mind in their homes for knowing that a certain threshold of living standards was being maintained.

Such a situation, with health and building codes all but unenforced for so long, was naturally lending the impression that anything went in the far-removed woodlands. While it was indeed always buyer beware, you'd've maybe thought your more sporting realtors might have posted the sobering reminder over their doorways.

People with enough resources to pay maybe $30,000 or more to put in a well and perhaps half again as much to get power lines extended, had enough to buy land — and more than any piddly two-and-a-half acres — with far easier water access and unencumbered by the endless squabbling of disaffected neighbors. Why would anyone spend so much to buy into such a discombobulated place?

Cheap land with million-dollar views only went so far.

CHAPTER 21

Early trouble in River City reconsidered

Most of Shasta Vista's two or three dozen founding families either knew each other from Southern California or would meet during their annual summer camp rendezvous. Couples ready to retire, they could easily afford to build code-legal residences and become instant lords and ladies of their own fledgling backwoods settlement. With the territorial imperative strong, many probably hoped to make — and keep — the one-time camp lands their own de facto rural retirement hideaway, let the chips fall where they may.

Too bad if it disappointed or angered those who'd bought parcels for camp retreat use. Or had wanted to build but waited too long to tap the limited power-and-light fund; you snooze, you lose. Or that investors now felt stuck with parcels no longer suitable for camping and too expensive to build on, becoming white elephant properties whose market was so sleepy it bordered on catatonic.

Theirs was a convention-minded culture. The alphas of the group held a buttoned-down, breezily urbane SoCal sensibility and a hell-for-leather law-and-order mindset. One that some might've viewed as a bit out of place at the top of more free-wheeling Northern California, even allowing for its location in a conservative neck of the woods. It struck more impressionable souls like me that an urbane L.A. culture had somehow been weirdly transplanted, fully intact, onto the top of the state's wild and woolly hinterlands. (But then, it wasn't unlike how, a half century later, an Asian American culture would quickly superimpose itself on the place, so maybe it wasn't that strange after all.)

In ways that counted, the Vista essentially became *their* place. Their tight-wound influence lingered for decades, long after the rabble began taking over the former would-be exclusive Xanadu. It would continue to shape the development's social climate and collective mindset through the old guard's efforts to salvage what remained of their one-time backwoods paradise and arrest further degradation.

The modern-day pioneers were angst-ridden over their place having lost its brief legitimate community status after the invasion by non-compliant dwellers. Unofficial duties suddenly expanded to include blowing the whistle to the county over any unapproved construction or overlong camp visits brought to their notice by their bloodhound cohorts, combing the maze of roads as if in search of escaped convicts.

Early on in the code-enforcement battle, desperate to pre-serve the endangered retirement haven, they rang the phones of Siskiyou County's Planning, Health, and Building Departments off the hook. Board members *demanded* the county hold the latest-discovered scofflaw's feet to the fire for trying to invade their law-abiding domain on the cheap — especially those with an infuriatingly taunting, *hee-hee-whadaryagointodoaboudit?* attitude that no doubt drove the blood pressure of many into the danger zone.

Bottomless cup of trouble

If enforcers failed to do their job and the culprits got away with it, it might amount to selective enforcement, grounds for a lawsuit against the county. So, for many years, the stretched-thin code enforcers had obliged, trying their damnedest to stamp out the scourge festering within the seemingly jinxed, would-be tranquil lands.

Then, at some point, they gave up. They'd ground their teeth to the gums addressing the perennial problem child with the relatively slim tax-generating base. One whose situation, no matter how much they tried to get a handle on it, proved to be a bottomless cup of trouble. Like a boat springing new leaks faster than one could plug existing ones, bailing was futile.

Of course, this seeming shirking of duty was deemed unacceptable by the heavily invested, tax-paying residents. Gone round the bend, they clung to the belief that strict enforcement of law and order could — *must* — save their new community from wrack and ruin. In seeming denial of the insurmountable challenges they faced with brazen code ignorers sprouting like hydra heads, their volunteer search parties kept blitzing, scouring the maze of roads, never-say-die, determined to run to earth any who dared be in the Vista while ignoring the residency requirements they deemed chiseled in stone.

With efforts in overdrive, posse members soon stopped

trying to even talk to the culprits and point out the error of their ways. Operations went covert. They'd no doubt tried earlier — some, no doubt, in a high-handed, imperious manner — then got huffy when told what they could do with their rules and regulations. Realizing they were dealing with a shameless, possibly violent, group of scofflaws who refused to respect authority, they began driving by furtively instead, stopping just long enough to scope the scene from the road and ascertain the lot's exact location. Later, they obtained the parcel assessment number from the master map index and filed a formal complaint for every last minutiae of noncompliance their painstaking efforts brought to light.

Sub-zero tolerance

It was for such a scorched-earth crusade that the unflattering moniker of "the gestapo" got bestowed on the board of directors by the Vista's more pragmatic, live-and-let-live residents. Some had gone through the compliance process wringer themselves or bought from those who had; they knew how hard it was to meet code for anyone wanting to live in the country and simplify their lives if on a modest income. They were shocked and dismayed that an ugly, sub-zero tolerance existed; playing such ruthless hardball didn't seem to go with living in the longing-to-be tranquil backwoods.

Even though the place was seriously derailing, people must've thought there surely had to be a better way to resolve matters. Maybe not, though. Not short of changing legal-residency regulations. Or suing the county for selective non-enforcement. Perhaps, for better or worse, it was simply the way things were. A cascading series of unfortunate events had locked residents into a state of perpetual conflict.

Living in denial

In time, the situation was so far gone that one might've thought the only thing left for the twisted-into-knots legal residents was to accept that their one-time paradise was history and try to make the best of it; the system they'd depended on and supported their entire lives had failed them. But that would've been too painful; these were to be their golden years, a carefree time after lifetimes of toil. So instead, they lived in denial. As dubious consolation, some took a certain grim satisfaction in making things as unpleasant as possible for any miscreants who dared to crash their party — even long after the party was a fading memory.

Sometimes they were successful in getting a few of the newer arrivals kicked out. Driving around the back roads of neighboring Section 13 in the nineties, one day I met a high-spirited man and his very pregnant partner in front of their remote parcel on Bounty Road. He'd just thrown up a tiny, makeshift two-story cracker-box palace of 2 x 4s and pressboard: instant home. A goat or two was grazing on the nearby sagebrush. I returned with a sense of foreboding a month or two later. Sure enough, they were gone. A bulldozer had leveled their shelter to the ground; the place looked like a tornado had hit it.

This was far from an isolated incident.

One might've said it was people's own fault for not doing better research. But some knew the score and had rolled the dice anyway, thinking it was such cheap land that it was worth a shot trying to end-run the system.

Bottom line: The fondest dreams of many would-be country dwellers of cultivating simple affordable living were obliterated during those trying times. Here and there, half-completed structures of varying ambition and construction levels stood forlorn, mute witnesses to their own disasters, abandoned and radioactive from code-violation busts, their builders having run out of cash, the will to comply, or both.

Over time, many would be picked off by the furtive lumber 'recyclers'. "Hey, it's just going to waste; I'm doing a service, doncha know." Such dubiously resourceful people considered any parcel fair game if it looked more abandoned than inhabited — that is, if there were no recent vehicle tracks at the entrance or vehicles parked on the property.

The place that at first had seemed easy come, easy go, often instead proved to be easy come, hard go.

Welcome to Mt. Shasta Vista: My first impressions

The large, imposing signs that were planted at each of the place's five county road entrances just beyond the welcome sign, plus at every section corner, made the board's policy crystal clear in large, bold, black print. The signs all but shouted:

**HEALTH AND BUILDING
CODES STRICTLY ENFORCED**

Woe betide any poor soul failing to heed such a no-nonsense warning.

So along comes this rambling, residence-shy 29-year-old nature boy of limited means in late 1978, burned out living on the road and nurturing a dream of building a bower in the wilderness. With champagne taste but a beer budget, I soon warmed to the notion of settling in the bone-dry, semi-wild, super-affordable juniper outlands instead of the redwood creekside of my dreams… to blasted code, if that's what it took, and as my limited resources and a steep learning curve allowed. Although it would prove by far the biggest project of my life up to then, at least lumber was still relatively cheap, and the building code a smidgen less onerous — if then rigorously enforced. I planned to join POWW's water-hauling group to avoid having to drill a well, which I couldn't have even *begun* to afford.

To my ridiculously impressionable mind, the growling entrance signs were of more than passing concern. Even if the lots were relatively affordable — most listed between $1,500 and $1,750 and some had easy terms of $250 down and $25 a month — the place struck me as more than a tad unfriendly. To me, the signage seemed to say: "Welcome to Mt. Shasta Vista; no this, no that, no the other thing under penal codes such and such; violators will be hanged by their toenails. In fact, we DARE you to even enter, bub."

Or, more concisely, "Welcome, now leave." Or, perhaps most to the point, like the scrawled-in-blood-red greeting sign posted on the outskirts of town in Clint Eastwood's Western revenge flick, *High Plains Drifter*: "Welcome to Hell."

On reading the top warning, in even bigger black lettering — "Private Property, Trespassers will be Prosecuted" — part of me felt like I might get arrested any second for having so foolishly entered, especially since it was after nightfall. I'd just driven over 300 miles and was too psyched to wait til morning to drink in the land. (My realtor had sent me a map circling a dozen parcels up for grabs.) I felt like I'd stumbled into some top-secret government compound and should turn around before it was too late. I imagined residents peeking out from behind their curtains and calling the sheriff to report a suspicious vehicle lurking about.

But, as was no doubt the case with countless land seekers of limited funds before and after me, cheap lot prices won out over due caution, eclipsing any first impressions screaming red alert.

Bad feng shui

Such sign wording, of course, had served many purposes. Yes, it was meant to discourage would-be substandard dwellings and, perish the thought, any white trailer trash, hop-headed bikers or scraggly longhairs like me from ever trying to invade their would-be respectable scene.

But it was also meant to dissuade wood poachers, unlicensed game hunters, trash dumpers, vehicle abandoners — and, in the earliest, vacation-only years, any miscreants harboring designs on plundering goods trustingly left on unfenced parcels. Even decades later, with hundreds of residents spread across the domain, a hulking 12 x 50-foot-long vacant mobile home was once boldly snatched in the dead of night from one lot and hauled over two miles to another without consequence.

They probably needed that loud bark, for all the good it did.

But the Chinese feng shui principle holds that the energy at a place's entrance creates a vibration that resonates throughout it. Sadly, the essence of such barking words indeed seemed to ripple throughout the realm, all the more so for being reinforced by similar huge signs at every section corner. Acquaintances visiting me decades later, as if wanting to play it safe and not risk someone towing their vehicle away, parked it forward of the baleful entrance sign and walked the entire 1.3 miles in.

That intriguing, welcoming wooden arch that once spanned the main entrance, seemingly filled with hope and promise? After being treated to my own 'unwelcome wagon' in due course, the cynic in me thought it might have just as well proclaimed:

ABANDON ALL HOPE
YE WHO ENTER HERE

CHAPTER 22

Doing the time warp again

It perhaps came as no surprise that the rigid attitude conveyed by the entrance signs was on full display at the monthly board meetings. Open to all parcel owners and family members, the proceedings, though dull as dishwater sometimes, were more often a caution. Gnarly shouting matches were not uncommon. At least once, a fistfight broke out on the floor.

It was as if the place had developed a deadly cancer; left untreated, it was fatally metastasizing. The tsunami waves of bickering among malcontent dwellers were so phenomenal, the place would've made rich fodder for the late gonzo journalist-author Hunter S. Thompson: *Fear and Loathing in the Vista.*

The first excited residents must've felt something akin to the firstcomer prospectors of California's 1849 Gold Rush. Briefly having the rich diggings to themselves, intoxicated with their great good fortune, things turned to pandemonium the instant a flood of fellow prospectors chasing the same yellow stone poured in.

Similarly (if nowhere near as dramatically or quickly), the earliest Vistan residents, beyond the occasional visiting camper, luxuriated in having the idyllic woodland domain all to themselves. They'd transplanted to the top of the state and were jealously guarded of the place, but had faith in local government to keep law and order intact. But, like the first miners, they got run over. Eventually, beside themselves with anguish, they became like so many mad King Lears, shouting imperious commands to the winds.

When less-solvent people first began moving in and dared to ignore health and building codes, the firstcomers still had the ball in their court. They'd established relations with county code enforcers and enjoyed a lock on board membership. They ran with the ball, clinging to it for dear life, dismissing as idiots anyone at meetings who took exception to their hardball tactics against the scofflaw intruders. Such people obviously didn't understand the dire gravity of the situation. Beyond desperate, their bottom line was that, come hell or high water, they'd dedicate themselves to keeping the county health and building codes enforced.

The alternative was unthinkable.

To arms, to arms

Desolated and shocked beyond endurance as the relied-on county enforcement began failing them, overwrought board members and their cohorts remained loaded for bear. With their dream village facing imminent ruination, they engaged in a desperate take-no-prisoners war of intimidation against every code ignorer they located — with or without county support. They must have thought that, through sheer will and collective determination and the knowledge that the law was on their side, they might at least stem the tide of further miscreants swamping their domain, and maybe some of the thorns in their sides would tire of the war of attrition and move on.

Steeled to win or go down fighting, for a while at meetings board members tried to dodge public discussion of hot-button issue proposals by steamrolling their "comply or else" agenda. They'd mumble, "public comments?" quickly out of the side of the mouth, like a crooked politician, before taking a fast vote: "Motion? … second? … all in favor … motion carried." They'd banked on newbies' unfamiliarity with formal meeting procedure. Shouts of protest once concerned newcomers got wise were countered by simpering yells from the board's supporters: "Robert's Rules! Robert's Rules!"

But despite their most valiant efforts, the well-heeled first-comers' dream of an idyllic backwoods retirement haven was turning into a nightmare; the Vista they'd known and cherished was being torn asunder before their eyes.

Tipping point

As more and more lot buyers of limited means settled in, bearing rebellious attitudes that rejected the idea of building *any*thing to code, the country's limited resources for enforcing the code reached a tipping point. Beyond it, they were unable to effectively impose the codes and ordinances (the very ones that people living in town, nowhere to hide, perforce toed the line on). This, despite, or perhaps because of, officials continually being apprised and updated on the intolerable situation by the apoplectic residency. Bees in their bonnets, they bugged them without letup over the latest-discovered infractions needing swift response. The idea of taking early retirement must've started looking good to some.

Over time, authorities all but abandoned code enforcement in the beset backwoods. One got the impression county officials liked to pretend it didn't exist (perhaps not unlike the place's outlaw dwellers' attitude towards their building ordinances). Except, again, for the property assessors' unfailing attention — eventually via satellite zoom-ins — to every parcel and what improvements, if any, were being made, to squeeze every possible shekel through the annual tax assessments.

Before authorities reached that tipping point, it seemed that the only responses aside from actual emergencies were to the more persistent calls from fuming parties who knew the law and possibly threatened legal action if they didn't respond. They became such pains that it was finally easier to drag themselves out and tell the culprits, "Hey, you can't be doing this, you'd better stop it, or else; we mean it," accompanied by a cold pointed stare, and hope the admonishment would stick.

Some scofflaws indeed at that point cleared out, having no stomach for unpleasant confrontations and their fantasies of cheap and easy country living having gotten clobbered to death. Others, thicker-skinned, kept on the way they were, almost as if daring them to try their damnedest. They felt that inertia, the long-enshrined sacredness of property rights, and the county's enforcement resources being spread thin would ultimately win the battle.

Eventually, they'd more or less prove themselves right.

White bread outpost

Though later early arrivals like me often felt nothing but scorn over the firstcomers' intolerance of certain others, in due time, long after getting settled, I couldn't help but sympathize with their plight. What a heartbreaking situation it must have been, seeing the place they'd invested so heavily in, doing everything by the book, nurturing fond hopes of enjoying the land they'd pioneered through their golden years, only to have it meet with such a rude awakening. The Vista could've, should've, would've been such a nicely settled, enviable, peaceable backwoods community of forthright, hail-fellow well-met, law-abiding residents…

… if only a white bread one.

While, at least in later years, absentee ownership appeared somewhat racially diverse — based on a 2014 scoping of the board's list of owners — the actual residency was overwhelmingly white. Though there were a few Hispanics and a Native American or two, there were no Black people to my knowledge, and only one Asian (Debbie, who, with her white husband Alex, had sued the board over the well closure). Having grown up in the polyglot melting pot of San Francisco, I didn't find anything too amiss about this, other than wincing whenever a neighbor dropped the 'n' word in casual conversation (and later, the 'c' word). I'd learned to adapt to any ethnic mix — or lack thereof — of a place, given an even playing field and an absence of expedient intentions.

The scene perhaps reflected rural Siskiyou County as a

whole, so predominantly white that it might've appeared, not without reason, as a narrow-minded, passively (sometimes overtly) racist backwater to any people of color arriving from large melting-pot cities that leaned towards a mutual racial tolerance and inclusivity born of everyday intercultural mingling over time.

Prejudice against Asian Americans aggravated by unlicensed seas of green

A more diverse Vista residency from the get-go might've made the would-be community culturally richer. But it was a moot point: Wonder Bread it was for a full half-century. Then, starting in 2015, residents of the mostly all-white world were shocked to find themselves suddenly surrounded by a flood of new, Asian American neighbors. People that some had probably never interacted with as equals were suddenly living right next door to them and down the road.

What caused the sudden influx? It soon became apparent that, with deep pockets and coordinated efforts, an ambitious campaign was in full swing to buy up the empty parcels by the hundred, homes too, with the intent of salvaging the largely failed subdivision and remaking it to suit themselves. Working together in overdrive with a tight sense of unity, they hoped to establish an instant rough-and-ready Asian American community…

…and, either unrealistically and or overboldly, hoped to support it by growing and marketing verboten seas of green.

It goes without saying that the mutual assimilation of races, often problematic, in Vista's case would've had a much better chance of succeeding without such massive illegal pot growing going on to over-complicate matters.

As residents and the surrounding community got up in arms over the undisguised open grows, the newcomers soon threw the race card into the mix. Of course, it was a justifiable charge; prejudice against Asians ran deep throughout United States history. But it now seemed to be used as a diversionary tactic to confuse and dilute issues, trying to leverage to one's advantage the awakening guilt of a white-dominated society, its systemic racism baked in so long that many had been in denial it even existed.

The charge indeed worked to divert attention away from the large-scale, audacious cultivation efforts underway as white people were left sputtering, "I'm not a racist." Their operations were so brazen that one Vista board member thought they surely *must* have obtained an ordinance variance to do what they were doing, or, obviously, they wouldn't be doing it. At first, growers tried to explain away the growth of so many plants by saying many needed massive amounts of cannabis buds for taking therapeutic soaks to effectively relieve the lingering pain of war-related injuries. No doubt, there was a kernel of truth in this, but lavishing a whole pound of bud for one therapeutic soak strained credulity to the breaking point.

Some might've viewed the efforts and explanations as magical thinking on a gigantic scale that defied and ultimately checkmated mundane realities.

Of course, similar scenes were happening all over California: unlicensed growers acting en masse, bold as brass, openly defying grow restrictions, as if daring anyone to say they couldn't. Sound the trumpets: In California, home of the Emerald Triangle and serious legal medical cannabis cultivation and underground networks supplying much of the nation for decades, the rogue growers' day had come at last.

An alternative scenario

One wonders how the course of the place might have gone if just as many Asians had moved here for other reasons, but instead built or bought code-legal homes and pursued legal livelihoods. Sure, there undoubtedly would've still been the same ugly reactions by any who demonized those of a different skin color. But once they'd either bailed or come around once healing their poisoned mindsets, residents would've worked through the initial mutual culture shock and, in time, gotten to know and appreciate each other.

Alas, that didn't happen. The inevitable result was a triple whammy: illicit scaled pot growing openly going on, prejudice flaring up, and the resulting severe erosion of civil order, the environment and tranquil country living.

Fine line

Anyone respecting the reasonable rule of law might hold that a development needed residents to work together on some level and to follow established rules to keep things safe and pleasant — the acid test being one's own children — so that everyone felt good about hanging their hats in the place. Otherwise, the weeds of civic indifference, unruly attitudes and shady goings-on could spring up, filling the social vacuum and choking a place's livability.

But on the other hand, it could make simple country living all but impossible if the rules were *too* strict, too expensive or too onerous for the majority of would-be residents to want to conform to.

In the Vista, there'd always been a fine line between having enough enforced rules and regulations to maintain a semblance of fair-minded civil order and having too many and courting sure rebellion. But developer Collins could never have gotten the place greenlit had he not set up the CC&Rs so that every buyer, by signing the legal title paperwork, effectively agreed to comply with every last applicable county, state, and federal rule, law and ordinance under the sun. (A disillusioned Vietnam War vet neighbor in the eighties, Aldrich Anderson, once told me, "The government makes liars, cheats and horse thieves out of everyone.")

No one around to say 'boo'

The rush of having one's own land in such a relatively remote region, under the often surreal sway of massive Mount Shasta, could easily obscure the reality of there being any such regulations *to* conform to. There wasn't anyone around to say 'boo' — especially after the county abandoned its residential code-enforcement in the budget-slashing move for some five years during the first half of the 2010s.

As respect for the rule of law waned, the likelihood grew that the Vista, its very reason for existing muddled and befuddled early on, its 1,000-plus big empty lots lying fallow for decades, would become irresistibly attractive to any chasing the lure of fast riches by openly growing lucrative cash crops of verboten weed. With recreational cannabis legalization around the corner and current enforcement laws losing their teeth, the time was right: The underground pot market was taking off to supply an insatiable jonesin' public for anyone willing to roll the dice.

Many would see the Vista, with its embarrassment of remote, forever-gone-begging, cheap-as-dirt parcels, as just what the doctor ordered. A full-throttle juggernaut was about to upend the entire sleepy backwoods hideaway.

———— CHAPTER 23 ————

Interlude: Highlights of my early years

'I say we got Trouble... with a capital 'T'

In early October 1978, I snapped up a two-level, gently sloping corner lot in Section 23's least inhabited uplands for $1,750, at $250 down and $25 a month. It had a staggering mountain view. That particular month, the national economy was experiencing the tightest dollar in ages. I think I came to value the land all the more because of this; it was a time when the dollar held extra-high value.

While I'd hoped to find land with water, there was excellent compensation for the place's obvious lack of it: *lots* of room to breathe. I remembered the American Indian advice: "Go to where there is no water, for that is the only place the white man will leave you alone."

I intentionally sought a parcel far from the blacktop. And as far from the few existing power lines as I could get. I wanted to live off the grid and knew someday I'd generate my own wind- or solar-power system. For 11 years I'd get by on kerosene lamps and candles and charging an extra 12-volt battery in my vehicle, before at last going solar in 1989, when panels cost about eight times what they would in 2025 — not even adjusting for inflation. (A 1 x 4-foot, 50-watt panel ran $400; factoring in 35 years of inflation, which drove up the average price of things about 2.5 times by 2025, that'd be like paying the equivalent of over $2,000 for a 100-watt panel that one might now grab as an impulse purchase at Harbor Freight.)

It was an early fall, and I scrambled to make camp. While days were still pleasantly sunny, overnight temperatures already plunged to a bone-chilling 13 degrees F. (-10 C.). I spent my first night shivering in my feather-leaking, down sleeping bag atop an Ensolite pad, set in a shallow trench, with plastic sheeting thrown over vertical sticks driven into the ground.

'You gotta permit for that?'

The next morning, I was heating water for coffee and trying to warm up over a small rock-lined campfire in a clearing 40 feet in from the road. I felt giddy and grateful to have my own land at last. Suddenly, an approaching pickup broke the silence that was becoming my new best friend. Its occupant, an older man, slammed on his brakes on spotting me. He wasn't part of the volunteer posse. Still, he was definitely wound up, the same as most every other compliant, year-round resident, I'd soon find out, who felt the place was in danger of being overrun by shiftless yahoos like me who needed telling what's what. He climbed out, stared at the campfire, and asked point-blank,

"You gotta permit for that?" Thus spoken were my first words of welcome from the would-be community before I could even enjoy my first sip of coffee.

They weren't encouraging.

Fast-forward six weeks, and I'd apparently waited too long to apply for a building permit — and, crucially, join the POWW water-truck club, rather than have to drill a well before qualifying for one once passing a perc test and digging an approved septic system. As a result, I got the full "Unwelcome Wagon" treatment from sundry busybodies of the peculiar development that, in my youthful haste to get my own land, I'd hitched my wagon to, determined to try to make the best of what might prove to be a sketchy living situation in a place that, I was fast learning to appreciate, was more than a skosh squirrelly around the edges.

Reluctant conformist

I'd intended to conform all along, if reluctantly, being an essentially timid, law-abiding soul, yet also possessed of a contrary, intellectually radical streak (perhaps only making me your typical walking human paradox). But I was gearing up slowly; it was a daunting prospect, building a house to code. Over the winter, I planned to research tiny home design, study construction methods and building codes, and fine-tune a plan to submit come spring. I was staying in the third-mile distant 12-by-16-foot cabin that a kindhearted neighboring couple, the Schumachers, had offered to let me winter in, out of the blue, in our first and only meeting. They'd been out for a walk, getting ready to leave as the pleasant-weather season wound down, and took pity on my situation.

This, so I wouldn't freeze to death trying to weather winter in my flimsy 10-by-16-foot Sears cabin tent, as I'd first resolved to do. I'd wanted to stay on my brand-new land and future homeland, no matter what. Cold alone I could endure with my accustomed spartan lifestyle, plus extreme-weather bedding and a jury-rigged wood stove for the tent (not recommended). I even had a pair of heavy-duty, super-insulated military-surplus pants once worn by airmen for Arctic jumps.

Unbeknownst to me, though, the region was notorious for its windstorms; they were so severe they beggared belief. Coming out of nowhere, they roared across the land like a runaway freight train; wind gusts of 70 to 80 mph were not uncommon. In the late 1980s, we'd get hit by a particularly severe storm, packing gusts of 100 mph; the Safeway in Weed reported its front glass blown in and 25-pound sacks of dog food airborne like so many feather pillows. Years later, while visiting my elderly neighbors, the Sheltons, I noticed some old wreckage lying in their yard and asked about it. "That's what's left of our old trailer," John said matter-of-factly. "A mini-twister got it. It used to be over there," he said, pointing a ways off. "You should've seen it sailing through the air."

December windstorms kept blowing my tent down no matter how hard I tried to secure the guy ropes. When it collapsed yet again in the middle of a howling blizzard one night, I finally gave up. Grateful I had the option, the next morning, my black cat, Cat, and I moved into the couple's vacated cabin. Thereafter, I made daily hikes to work on my place, clearing brush, roughing in a roadway, and building an earth-sheltered shed that would become my legal onsite construction shelter once I secured an all-important building permit.

On my trail

Before I could get it, though, I seemed destined to experience the full wrath of my unknown neighbors and their absolute intolerance of anyone not doing things strictly according to Hoyle. It appeared that ever-vigilant Vista board members and their cohorts had established a pipeline with local realtors for every Vista parcel sale. My so-called neighbors, most living several miles off, learned how yet another rambling upstart of apparent threadbare means had dared to invade their would-be respectable realm, doubtless with no intention of ever paying the piper. My Strout Realty seller gave me the heads-up. He said that while he'd admitted selling a lot to a certain young man, he wouldn't say who or where.

I found that sporting of him.

But now a determined posse was hot on my trail. They systematically combed the endless backroads, determined to run me to earth, along with any others they might stumble across. (My "you-gotta-permit-for-that" neighbor, to his credit, hadn't reported me; he turned out to be a decent guy named Seburn.) Weeks later, they finally discovered my lair while I was away in town. They'd taken one look at my thrown-together, mostly underground structure (then strictly a storage shed), plus my verboten outhouse, and rushed to report me to the Siskiyou County Health Department. They didn't know, or, I suspect, care, that I had every intention of complying and building to code. (Again, it wasn't that I particularly *wanted* to — I'd've preferred building a free-form underground home — but I valued peace of mind and knew I'd never experience it if I didn't toe the line.)

Their scorched-earth policy allowed no wiggle room; I'd already been on the land longer than the 30-day-a-year rule allowed. Equal opportunity hasslers, anyone non-compliant — especially those they didn't cotton to as not their kind — were zealously reported to authorities as if they'd discovered the hideout of one of the FBI's Ten Most Wanted.

Busted

I was duly summoned on the carpet of the then-head county health department honcho, Dr. Bayuk, who'd just capped the truck club's membership, newly determined to make every other lot owner bring in a well before becoming eligible for a building permit. No doubt smarting from a wrathful earful he'd endured over this latest upstart's audacity, I was given the bum's rush. But then, oddly, he offered me an out, if grudgingly: He'd give me 120 days to get into make-shift compliance by digging and installing a septic system, even though I wouldn't have a completed cabin to connect it to for years, and then build a temporary outhouse over it to use in the meantime. Otherwise, he said, he'd see to it that I'd be thrown off my land by the sheriff. "And don't think I won't!" he growled, jowls shaking like Nixon's. He no doubt felt I needed an extra dose of fear to get me properly motivated.

It turned out that at the last moment, another kindhearted neighbor, Mrs. Norton, had come forward on my behalf and explained to him how they'd promised to let me join POWW once I was ready to build. He thus allowed me to slip in and become the water-truck group's 26th and last member.

Being thin-skinned, the entire experience traumatized me. It happened within months of arriving bursting with excitement at the prospect of at last fulfilling a decade-long dream of having my own land. Despite the last-minute reprieve, at first I felt like giving up on the place that, it was now abundantly clear seethed with some unfathomably intense, dark spirit of intolerance that bordered on spooky.

Devastated and demoralized, part of me felt like I was about to again fade away into a cold, cruel world. (Being homeless can be an amazingly effective dispiriter. Some say people become homeless because they have a mental illness, but often it's *being* homeless that makes otherwise-functional people start to lose it.) Though my fondest hopes and dreams had been mangled, the wind taken from my sails, I dredged up reserve willpower from somewhere. With the resilience of youth, I became newly determined to make the best of a lamentable situation.

I paid the $125 water-truck membership fee and was set to invest whatever time, money and effort it took to get legally squared away. Then I'd at least be able to live on the land with a modicum of dignity and hopefully salvage my poet's dream of building a bower in the wilderness. This, while doing my level best to tune out those who seemed to live to give others grief, due to, as I'd later appreciate, their *own* fondest dreams having been so savagely mauled by the vicious circle of intolerance by locals wreaking havoc on the land when *they* arrived.

Green light

I passed the perc test, and dug and installed the approved septic system. As per the agreement, I built an outhouse over the tank once it and the leach field passed inspection and were backfilled. In part for the benefit of any busybodies driving by to check out the scene of the troublemaker's almost-bust (*damn, I thought sure we had him*), no doubt hoping to find some new reportable offense, I painted on the side facing the road, in big bright blue letters: "Welcome Halley's Comet in 1984." *That should baffle 'em.* Then I built another outhouse more to my liking, set farther in, and used it until I moved into the completed cabin, years later. It was a low-slung squatter affair cleverly disguised as a doghouse, with a water bowl and leash in front, and a piece of plywood and large cushion over the opening. No one ever discovered the ruse.

Over a leisurely three-and-a-half-year period, I built a code-approved cabin. It was a one-and-a-half-story, solar-tempered, shed-roofed, open-beam, big-tiny home (625 square feet). Although I was required to fully wire the structure for 110-V electrical, I was off the hook for connecting to the grid because I was beyond the mandatory-hookup distance.

Meanwhile, I lived 20 feet away in my tiny semi-underground hobbit home, a cozy 8-by-12-footer. On the door — made of old planks I'd salvaged from far-gone ruins of the one-time stagecoach rest station below Sheep Rock (they had square nails, phased out around 1890) — I posted a Shakespeare quote from *Hamlet*:

> *"I could be bounded by a nutshell and*
> *count myself a king of infinite space…"*

I used only hand tools, wanting the building experience to feel intimate and relaxed. I had energy to burn, being in my prime. I hired help for the open-beam roof, meeting Jack Yerke, a professional carpenter, while scrounging at the Weed dump. For a modest fee, he agreed to guide the roof work, which involved manually lifting up into place eight 20-foot, 4 x 10 rafter beams, each weighing over 200 pounds. (I scrounged for reusable lumber at various dumps and the town's Opportunity Center whenever possible.) And I hired an older handyman from Dunsmuir to show me the ropes of wiring to code.

It appeared I was on the verge of becoming a quasi-respectable resident. Not that I was any longer interested in being accepted as such by the place's league of dedicated busybodies and certified hasslers. It was like the classic Groucho Marx quip, made over a restrictive country club offering him a membership despite his being Jewish: "I didn't want to belong to any club that would have me as a member." It'd be decades before I'd warm up to the board and appreciate its *potential*, at least, to do good for the floundering, perpetually at odds with itself, rural community that I'd thrown in with.

Working under the gun of the county code enforcers and soon getting paranoid — I imagined them trading notes with wary Vista board members and cohorts on request — proved so depressing, it drove me to drink (beer and wine). I was learning firsthand how board members and their ilk had a talent for radicalizing the place's denizens in their abortive efforts to try restoring it to its former genteel glory. Or, barring that impossible dream, and as an abject, warped-out consolation, demand a pound of flesh by giving holy hell to anyone who dared be in the Vista without hewing to every last rule and regulation.

At times, it felt as though the place were eternally locked in its own little contention-drenched time warp.

On the wings of getting my new shelter signed off in

early 1983 (total cost: $13,500), I was a timid if rebellious 33-year-old who was now well familiar with and thoroughly disenchanted by the place's imperious would-be overlords.

Rainbow family welcomes the Vista home

So naturally I got myself into even bigger trouble. It seems I decided to celebrate the return of Halley's Comet by hosting a months-long rainbow family camp on my land.

In 1984, the annual national rainbow gathering, with participants' countercultural vision of living together in peaceful harmony on the land (if only for one week a year) was going to be held in California for the first time since its inception 12 years earlier in Colorado. It would be happening in an area two hours distant, in the Warner Mountains wilderness, a ways from the towns of Alturas and Likely, in the state's remote northeast corner. Come spring, a flood of psyched early-comers, some returning for the first time in decades to their new age roots, would be pouring in from everywhere, including overseas. Many would have nowhere to go until the precise public forest site was chosen, still months away.

I wanted to reconnect with my roots after 15 years adrift from my hometown of San Francisco, with its once-rich hippie counterculture, while evening the ledger for the countless people who'd helped me during my years of endless hitchhiking and riding the rails. I realized I'd be helping liberate the often dreary, fuddy-duddy development in the process. Come February, I would open my land to all comers for what would turn out to be an eventful five months destined to shake loose the place more than I'd hoped.

Even as the Vistan firstcomers had built their homes amidst a de facto recreational development, seemingly unmindful of the troubles their move might create for the over 1,000 other lot holders, I was equally determined to let the chips fall where they may for hosting a motley group of merry refugees from conventional living — people whose lifestyle was the very antithesis of my law-and-order fellow inhabitants of Impossible Acres.

Party-hearty space travelers

I solemnly tendered my invitation by letter to the rainbow steering committee, which was holding its monthly steering committee sessions in the city hall chamber (of all places) of faraway Chico. Word spread fast, and though it would never be recognized as an "official" rainbow camp for being held on private land, for months hundreds of wired earlycomers — often in colorful, glad-rag garb and driving outlandish rigs — traipsed in and out of the buttoned-down-and-proud Vista hinterlands like so many party-hearty space travelers vacationing from another galaxy. In a way, the scene came to feel like the animated feature *Yellow Submarine*, where the Beatles' triumphantly happy music turns the bleak, frozen, black-and-white world into dazzling technicolor.

Rainbow elders Whitney Loman and Richard Eagle Feather oversaw the setup of their three 28-foot yurts — formerly belonging to the Seattle region's controversial Love Family spiritual commune sect — on the parcel's lower back acre. "There's your UFO, Stuart!" someone shouted as the central yurt went up; earlier, I'd mentioned how I once liked to imagine a scout ship someday landing on my parcel. I'd even named my place Earthbase, a whimsical homage to a former Seattle Capitol Hill fire station that had been repurposed as a community center and renamed Earth Station. My place was thereafter referred to as Earthbase for years, even after I stopped letting friends hang out here, as I needed to reclaim the space for personal healing.

Of course, the rainbow gathering (technically only a pre-seed camp) wasn't all peace and love... far from it. Off-putting power plays, ego trips, and less-than-understanding attitudes erupted regularly, people being people and the eighties being trying times. And dyed-in-the-wool rainbows were hard-pressed to gear up full-tilt into their absolute-freedom mindset on private land rather than the accustomed public forest land. Even so, the place often overflowed with incredibly juiced and transcendent energies. I had to work triple time to get into the flow of things after having lived alone for so long, and needed to detach from ownership of the place as best I could if I hoped to feel one among rather than some impossible landlord.

Royal conniption fit

When my convention-locked neighbors heard what that Ward was up to now, they naturally had a royal conniption fit. Though a few more liberal-minded retirees would seem tickled by it all — possibly themselves rebels at heart and not seeing anything too threatening about the surreal scene — others were beside themselves. No wild, uncouth long-hairs, with their insufferable, flagrant pot smoking (then very much illegal), shameless public nudity, and unsettling tribal drum jams pounding far into the night in their one-time Elysian Fields now going to rack and ruin, dammit. One family per parcel; that was a Vista rule etched in stone. (Reminding them that "We *are* one family" wouldn't cut much ice.)

Frothing at the mouth, they reported me to every enforcement agency they could think of: county sheriff, health, planning and building departments, fire marshal, forestry… But, saving grace, earlier on I'd coordinated a meeting between then-sheriff Charlie Byrd and the rainbow elders, held on my land in what was designated the prayer-and-meditation yurt. Law enforcement was keen to learn what they might expect with some 33,000 (as it would turn out) rainbow celebrants soon to invade their turf. I laughed out loud when one irate resident later demanded to know whether the event was going to be held on my parcel. (A surreal image flashed through my mind, as one brought on by the question, "How many angels can dance on the head of a pin?")

The sheriff — at least tenuously reassured our ragtag group appeared to be a basically harmless if freaky bunch, beyond the obvious pot smoking and nudity, likely to only cause a temporary glitch in the conventional order of things — must've told my apoplectic neighbors to chill out a while and grit their teeth, it'd soon be over.

Jaws surely must've dropped; the damn system was failing them yet *again*.

Of course we're occult

Local TV station KTVL Channel 10, based in Medford, Oregon, sent a reporter and cameraman to capture footage our group and interview Eaglefeather, our ad hoc media spokesperson. He was decked out in his rainbow finest and in rare form, answering questions in the yurt with a deliberate thoughtfulness. When the reporter asked him, "Are you occult?" I thought, "*Well, of course we're occult; we're into astrology, numerology, metaphysics…*" But I'd misinterpreted the question, as I realized when I watched the segment aired later that week. It was, of course, a snarky, "Are you a *cult*?" query. In a half-hour interview, they used only about 10 seconds of Eaglefeather speaking. (He'd pointed out that the event would bring in lots of extra business.) Those challenging the long-entrenched social paradigm by living differently always made people uneasy, as if they were being forced to question its validity.

I went on the road for a month in June with my girlfriend, Peaches, who was meeting her sister in Indianapolis before flying to visit their brother stationed in Germany. While I was gone, irate neighbors came by, demanding to see me and no doubt hoping to intimidate me into pulling the plug on the scene, then four months along. Whitney was one of the most forthright men I'd ever met. I later heard he'd confronted them like a lion of Judah, reading *them* the riot act for giving me such a hard time that my pregnant girlfriend (by her last boyfriend) and I had to leave to get some peace. (It wasn't strictly true, but it got to them.) He demanded to know why they couldn't just let it be. He spoke straight from the heart, no doubt fixing them with such an intensely earnest look, as was his way, that it left them feeling chagrined and perhaps never so righteously rebuked in their lives.

Rebellious offspring and grandkids of the outraged residents, visiting to score some pot, soak in the vibes and ogle the casual nudity, loved it. The camp became Vista lore (what little there was of it). A mostly free-spirited half-year happening, it served to loosen the stranglehold of the place's long-oppressive regime. People breathed a little easier. Maybe it did so at the risk of encouraging an anarchistic spirit to gain *too* strong a foothold in the former, depressingly strait-laced community. Maybe not. It was hard to say.

It seemed that over the decades the place could swing from one extreme to the other: from the firstcomers' honeymoon period, happy campers giddy over the endless possibilities of their new pristine properties; to a ruthless law-and-order-minded, "No nothing, we mean it" regime by the first residents; then back to "Whoopee, anything goes!" spirit, if perhaps now on a bit more relaxed, more diverse, more live-and-let-live level.

The place was a chameleon, changing into whatever the majority of its current residents wanted. Or a chimera: a bizarre hybrid of opposing energies cobbled together like some improbable mythological beast.

CHAPTER 24

Locals gone wild

The long-ago firstcomers' overwound control-freak stance, replete with barking signs everywhere, had been, again, born of the earlier, urgently felt need to protect the place and vacationers' belongings while living 700 miles away 11 months of the year. Mischief-minded offspring of embittered locals who'd taken strong exception to the takeover of their former stomping grounds had a hell-for-leather field day during their long absences. This, of course, got the latter spitting nails mad on their return, their hoped-for carefree vacations, anticipated all year, met with a rude awakening: Their beloved new hideaway was being violated, their belongings vandalized and stolen.

Outcome: They were already seriously bent out of shape years long before the code scoffers ever showed up.

The locals — some maybe fourth- or fifth-generation descendants of the region's pioneers and deeply set in bucolic ways — were worlds away from welcoming the big-city-based, parcel-buying newcomers who seasonally invaded their closed-off backwoods. The least charitable mounted what was

253

basically a pitched, *"You may think it's your land, but it's still ours; we'll never recognize your damn place"* campaign. It lasted decades. Some might say it's still going on. The endless miles of non-gated, groomed back roads had been irresistibly inviting to the region's mischievous kids on their dirt bikes for gouging deep donuts in the freshly poured, sometimes deep, cinder topping, while older, more delinquent-minded youth had engaged in more serious hell-raising and outright thievery.

The need for fences wasn't felt

So it was that unruly youth — having absorbed the deep upset of their elders and coming to their defense, as it were — had geared up a protracted war with the well-heeled invaders who'd dared to commandeer their favorite hunting, grazing and kegger-partying land. Law enforcement had limited capacity to work with absentee owners, and only a few people oversaw the seven square miles of ungated entrances and 1,641 unfenced lots during their extended absences.

Over the decades, the eventual Vista residents often never even fenced their estates, perhaps at most setting a few rocks beside the bordering road or fashioning some other "friendly" fence; the place had seemed so tranquil and protected, at least while they were there, that the need hadn't been felt. The problem was that the actual landowner had to file an incident report to start any investigation, and some belongings, no doubt, went missing over half a year before the owners realized it.

By the time parcel holders started living here, it might have seemed too late to mend relations with the longtime locals. As in a tradition-bound Japanese village, they were deemed perpetual outsiders for not having been born here. Not even after they'd merged with the larger community, attending church services and, later, as a tiny number of younger families moved in, enrolled their kids in the local schools and joined the PTA. The longstanding vicious circle continued spinning round, perhaps fading a little with each passing year as more and more new people moved into the region. But it was still there, locked in the multi-generational residents' social DNA. Dislike and suspicion of the development and its invasive lot owners and their progeny appeared to be permanently ingrained in the old-time locals, their kids, their grandkids…

And all this happened, again, ages before the flocks of code-scoffing back-to-the-landers trickled in, or, generations later, the sea of unlicensed pot growers flooded the place.

Mt. Shasta Vista and its inhabitants were, all along, persona non grata in the eyes of most locals.

'Permit? We ain't got no permit...
I don't need no stinkin' permit!'

Throughout the 1980s and 1990s, the county fitfully enforced its health and building ordinances. Unless one didn't mind being deemed an outlaw and never earning recognition and acceptance as a legal resident — and in time, more and more wouldn't mind at all — landowners wanting to live on their parcels complied as a matter of course. Or at last gave the appearance of complying: "See here? I started my well; I'm 50 feet down and waiting on my next paycheck to drill deeper; cut me some slack here, okay?" *Good, I think he might be buying this.*

During the Great Recession of 2008-2009 that devastated the global economy, county supervisors were forced to make some tough calls. Among other measures, they axed the position of residential-code enforcer, which seemed to be having so little effect anyhow, leastwise in the Vista, a lost cause if ever there was one.

Over the next half-decade, residential-code enforcement essentially disappeared from Mt. Shasta Vista as if it never existed.

With no official telling you anything different, it was easier than ever for a newcomer to foster the illusion that one could do whatever they wanted on their lots with little fear of consequence. The old threatening signs were by then seriously biodegrading, dire warnings fading into illegibility. They lent the place the air of a forlorn, rural semi-ghost town living out its peculiar zombie half-life in sleepy obscurity.

No legal power to fine; liberty vs. license

Other subdivisions forming in the region about the same time apparently sought to ensure they established and maintained a respectable, law-abiding residency. Accordingly, they gave the property owner boards the legal power to levy fines for violations of agreed-upon rules. If not paid, they could put a lien on a culprit's property, which had to be cleared before the land could legally change hands. In nearby Lake Shastina, visible clotheslines, solid fencing and dirt bikes were all verboten. In the McCloud area's Shasta Forest, one could be fined $50 for changing oil on one's own property even if every drop was captured for recycling.

No such legal powers ever existed in Mt. Shasta Vista.

This has always been the place's two-edged sword. While its relative lack of sometimes nitpicky, overreaching rules and regulations empowered residents to feel more like lords and ladies of the manor, as it were, such freedom could obviously also attract scofflaws. Example: The place long ago had a monumental eyesore in a lower section: wall-to-wall junk, largely automotive, surrounded by undisturbed bordering wooded lots, like a junkyard had been surreally plopped in the middle of pristine woods. It took the board ages to get the county to condemn it and demand that the owner clean up the place.

In a democracy, it always came down to giving people the freedom to do whatever they wanted so long as it didn't interfere with the rights of others to do whatever *they* wanted. Liberty vs. license. The flip side of liberty was, of course, the obligation to support the rules of law set up to safeguard the freedom rights of the majority: the greatest good for the greatest number. The fact that the rules sometimes seemed to favor the interests of the wealthier at the expense of the less fortunate, who often seemed to get the short end of the stick, was doubtless what made people want to rebel against the system in the first place.

Can a place get centered without a center?

As mentioned earlier, not many Vistan parcel holders — either absentee owners or residents used to going it alone — ever felt the need for a community center. Even though its population had grown enough to merit one, there was never enough interest in establishing a place where residents and visiting lot owners could meet and get to know each other in a neutral, relaxed setting and form informal volunteer action groups like community gardens and litter patrol, hold swap meets — and have monthly board meetings on actual Vista land rather than next door in a tiny, borrowed, cold-fluorescent-lit fire station's backroom.

But indeed they were long held in that cramped, seasonally chilly backroom. And the annual property owner meeting? For many years, it was held 12 miles away in Lake Shastina. One had to walk through the golf club's bar lounge, often littered with schnockered tee enthusiasts, to reach the conference room. In earliest years, they were held *hundreds* of miles away, at places like many members' favorite at the time, the Madonna Inn, in San Luis Obispo. The board had wanted to make it easy for the many Southern California owners to attend. This shows the substantial influence South State lot holders held during the place's formative years.

At the risk of stating the obvious, it was difficult for a quasi-community to find its center without having a center. Leave the place for monthly meetings and drive 12 miles away for annual meetings? It didn't compute. While it struck more than a few as weird, the situation was perhaps only par for the course with the place's noteworthy degree of wrongheaded discombobulation.

'Wouldn't give you a dime...' vs. 'Only $29,999!'

Because of the place's sundry shortcomings, the sale values of parcels stalled for decades; prices barely kept pace with inflation. The lack of interest in the lots took the meaning of 'soft market' to new lows: Until 2015, unimproved two- to three-acre parcels went ignored at $5,000. Lacking any easier water, sewage, electricity or a more can-do, fair-minded and empowered board to keep things on even keel, the development all but screamed: "Beware! Failed subdivision!"

The place was so sketchy, it struck few as a promising place to want to drop anchor, or at least not for long. But subsets of land hunters were attracted to it: those with maybe an austere streak, who might actually enjoy roughing it a while, or those determined to live on the cheap, who wouldn't lose any sleep over being non-compliant, "Screw the system" being their motto.

Also, those renting houses and mobiles from code-compliant owners who'd moved away, for affordability more than anything, and then tried their best to tune out the place's glaring defects. And those few who, while maybe aware of its shortcomings, ventured to build a code-legal home anyhow, hoping the pluses would outweigh the minuses in the long run. And those who'd known the place in kinder times and invested so much time and effort to establish their residences that they were braced to weather changes that had others fleeing in a heartbeat.

Long ago, I met a former realtor who said, with a disdain apparently held in certain local property-peddling circles, "I wouldn't give you a *dime* for any of them!" He said this with such fire-breathing intensity, you might've thought the development was built over a toxic waste dump. It made me wonder whether he and his colleagues had skirted ugly lawsuits and been accused of misrepresenting a property's status, or endured some other unpleasantness that made it not worth the paltry commission fees the sale of such problematic, low-end properties might've brought.

Eventually, two out-of-region realtor groups, perhaps not knowing any better, tried fresh approaches. Specializing in scouting for rural developments deemed undervalued, in the late 2000s they snapped up hundreds of the bedeviled hinterland parcels, in the process at long last relieving many long-stuck owners. They mounted slick sales campaigns to remedy an obviously under-exploited situation, intent on making a mint through fast turnover and high markup.

'The Ponch' pitches parcels

The first outfit was National Recreational Properties, Inc. It hired former "CHiPs" TV star Erik Estrada as uber-aggressive pitchman. Out of Irvine (possibly the same town as Vista founder Collins), it apparently had a penchant for going after failed, "left-for-dead" subdivisions as easy prey, sharp talons squeezing out what quick profit they could before swooping off to the next rural roadkill. In their ad promos, "the Ponch" enthused how the place was so great he even owned a parcel. (Of course, he was given it just so that he could say that.)

The outfit reportedly offered to fly prospective buyers in to enjoy a champagne brunch, along with the big pitch and a grand tour of the prime affordable properties that offered such enviable solitude, fresh air and dazzling mountain views. But when they held the grand open house, helium balloons festooning highway entrances, rumor had it that no one even showed up. (They were more successful with their Alturas, California area development, California Pines, which boasted over *15,000* one-acre parcels. Though, for some unfathomable reason, it demanded the installation of super pricey, individually engineered septic systems, hindering *its* development.)

Campgrounds for the homeless?

A few years later, around 2012, the other group, BillyLand. com, grabbed a similar mess of raw Vista parcels, possibly taking some off the former's hands. They, in turn, appeared to be aiming at the less real estate-savvy, more easily snookered, and reckless, land-hungry Internet surfer crowd: They hawked the parcels online, eBay-style. The "winner" was the one who'd made the highest down-payment bid when the timer ran out. Buying land sight unseen with a few simple clicks and no credit checks… Such an idea's time had apparently come. "Only $29,999!" they gushed. (I probably would've fallen for it myself 34 years earlier.)

Of course, with low monthly payments and high interest rates, the ultimate cost could exceed $50,000. Predictably, their campaign attracted many living on a shoestring. The three BillyLand lot buyers I met were all soon growing cannabis plants, no doubt in part to try keeping up the monthly payments and avoid losing what some legal residents uncharitably deemed to be little more than private campgrounds for the homeless.

80 code-legal residences amid 1,641 lots

At the start of 2015, according to county records, the Vista had 80 approved residences. That meant that out of 1,641 parcels, roughly one in 20, or five percent, held site-built homes or brought-in mobiles and modulars that met code. The rest — some 1,556 lots, or 95% — either had non-permitted dwellings, were once informally lived on and since vacated, or, most often, were as pristine as the day the place was launched a half century earlier. (Minus, of course, scars of tree poachers and off-roaders, abandoned trailers and windblown detritus generously donated by residents of upwind lots.)

But hope sprang eternal for the various speculative landholders forever intent on trying to wrangle some profit from the clunkers. Some set overblown prices on their lots when listing them, thinking to snag an eager, uninformed buyer with more dollars than sense, oblivious to their depressed market value and the development's insidious doom loop. "Secluded," "That perfect spot to build your dream house," "a slice of heaven," the realtors enthused as shamelessly as bold streetwalkers asking passersby, "Wanna date?"

In the early teens, the sale of a lot in Section 13 to a conventional-minded woman was about to close. She was taking one last look at the parcel before signing. A nearby longtime scofflaw resident, Sean Miller, was determined to keep out his *own* "wrong kind of people." He strode out into her view buck naked and pranced about entirely for her benefit.

The ploy worked; the deal fell through.

CHAPTER 25

'Maybe if we ignore them,
they'll go away'

It was no great secret that the county supervisors rued the day they ever greenlit what became such a gloriously problematic development. Former Vista board president stalwart Jeannette Hook, who often met with county officials in the course of her work, said they viewed Mt. Shasta Vista as "the red-headed stepchild no one knew what to do with."

Although the place was entirely at the mercy of county officials to keep intact whatever shreds of respect for the rule of law remained, the vast, mostly rural county, on an over-stretched budget, had of course long ago given up trying to deal with it. Enforcement and policy-making parties grew so numb to the perpetual thorn in their side that they discon-nected from the inconvenient truth that its legal residency paid the property taxes funding their salaries and rightly expected them to earn their keep.

Despite — or because of — the number of non-compliant

dwellers flourishing, it seemed authorities were increasingly unwilling to respond to requests for help short of an actual emergency. One would think they must've appreciated the growing likelihood that the place was an even greater disaster waiting to happen. But even if so, what could they do? Authorities couldn't drive on its private roads without cause or formal permission from the Vista board, and the association would've probably had to pay higher annual assessments to fund such patrols, so that was a nonstarter. Besides, as bad as things were, it seemed many didn't want deputies cruising about, reminding them of the trying urban scene they'd left behind; people would deal with the challenges of their new rural surroundings as best they could on their own and hope for the best.

Things had gone wrong so long that the place baffled and bewildered most everyone, perhaps none more so than its residents. It was a strange beast that had somehow gotten away with defying many of the "normal" world's rules and regulations and was now experiencing the unpleasant consequences. Residents shrugged, feeling it was beyond saving. Countless absent lot holders, in turn, indifferent to the place's crying needs, knew only that they wanted out as soon as possible without losing their shirts. And officials, for their part, kept kicking the can down the road, coasting on autopilot, determined to avoid dealing with the wayward backwater whenever humanly possible...

... until the great day of reckoning came at last.

A tidal wave of instant-community builders and fortune seekers discover the Vista

I was taking a stroll along my road one day in the winter of 2014-2015 when I noticed several long-slumbering, unfenced vacant lots had received fresh attention. New surveying posts were planted with scrawled bearings and Day-Glo ribbons fluttering off their tops — no doubt just like at the start of the subdivision a half century earlier.

There they go again, I thought dismissively. *Realtors, still trying to sell the unsellable. Will they never learn?* Then, over the next few days, I noticed similar survey flags and boundary sticks planted along my regular driving route. I started to wonder. It seemed *some*thing was going on, but what? Was some new back-to-the-land movement afoot? Was a developer building a major attraction nearby that would make people suddenly want to live here? Had gold been discovered?

I tried putting it out of my mind and stuck with my initial conclusion: It was only the latest half-baked realtor campaign to entice a new crop of ill-informed land shoppers to part with their hard-earned money for all but useless parcels.

Baffling sound

Then, several weeks later, I awoke to the persistent sound of metal striking metal.

Perplexed, I stepped out to the porch. Actually, the noise seemed to be coming from several directions at once. It sounded as if a surreal flock of persistent metal woodpeckers had descended on the region and were rat-a-tatting up a slow-motion storm. Walking out to the front of my driveway, I saw a slight Asian man about forty yards off, pounding a metal T-post with focused determination, preparing to string barbed wire along it to other posts.

This was a peculiar and unsettling sight in a place whose lot owners often never put fences around their actual *residences*, let alone barbed-wire ones around *empty lots*. I had no idea what to think. (Yes, the obvious often escaped me.) I felt a vague uneasiness, a sinking feeling, a dread sense of foreboding. But I didn't feel compelled to walk over and introduce myself to find out what was going on. (I got to know him later; his name was Bonsai —my phonetic spelling — and he turned out to be an interesting man.)

A few days later, a small party of what sounded to be white people was talking among themselves on the corner lot across from me. Not used to hearing voices so close by in my remote neck of the woods, curiosity at last led me to walk over and try to find out what the heck was going on. Naively, I'd hoped they might be new homesteaders planning to build, as they were busy pacing off an area. But they were evasive, as if they'd rather not even talk to me. I couldn't understand why. Out of the blue, mistakenly thinking I *surely* knew what they were up to, one blurted, "We're not bad people." This, of course, only further mystified me.

Big *duh*

Over the following weeks, I noticed barbed-wire fencing was going up everywhere — along with "No Trespassing" and "Posted: Private Property" signs — around lots that had been vacant for generations. Finally, as I vaguely remembered how, driving through next-door's Juniper Valley development a year or two earlier, I'd seen many of its lots similarly fenced off with barking signs and realized what was happening *there*, it dawned on me: People were now snapping up *Vista's* cheap parcels to grow pot on… lots of pot on… lots and *lots* of pot on.

All illegally.

Slam dunk

California would be once again gearing up to vote on legalizing recreational cannabis in next year's November election through Proposition 64. Another proposition *almost* passed six years earlier. (The very first proposition, 19, had been voted down *44* years earlier, in 1972.) This time it was a guaranteed slam-dunk.

Enough signatures to put the proposition on the ballet would come about by May 4, 2016, but it'd be a long time before new cultivation regulations and restrictions rolled out. Pot dispensaries wouldn't open until over a year after the following year's election, on January 1, 2018, almost two years away. The populace's appetite for getting stoned was growing keener with legalization just around the corner, plus more and more were getting into cannabis's natural healing virtues for various health issues over Big Pharma's sometimes dubious laboratory concoctions, with their sobering "may-cause-death" disclaimers.

Those in the know realized a ginormous, once-in-a-lifetime window was opening. Growers who jumped the gun and were willing to go outlaw could easily grow and sell literal tons of bud underground to the underserved, pot-jonesin' and natural-healing seeking population, both in California and beyond, especially in states where even medical marijuana remained illegal.

After California became the first in the nation to legalize medical cannabis but then long resisted legalizing its recreational use, the line between the two blurred. A massive groundswell of rebellion sprang up, growing stronger with each passing year. Eventually, Washington State, Colorado, Alaska, Nevada and Washington, D.C. legalized it. But not California. Finally, knowing legalization was imminent in the state, emboldened growers decided to go for it, daring to openly defy the laws on the books to supply a select insatiable public wanting to either get high and enjoy a mini-vacation from mundane reality, or to utilize cannabis in genuine medical use. With legalization a sure thing, they knew existing pot laws would be rapidly losing their once-formidable enforcement teeth. They were like a lame-duck president whose authority all but vanished as election day approached.

A monumental open rebellion of unlicensed pot growing was gearing up to go full-tilt boogie in California.

'There's gold in them thar buds!'

Word spread that countless remote banana-belt Vista lots were for sale dirt-cheap. No doubt this was in large part because the former Vista board president's real estate outfit knew what was in the wind. They'd rushed to mount a massive marketing campaign in the poor rural county that would likely be late out the gate, lagging behind neighboring counties in passing restrictive ordinances and getting a handle on soon-to-unfold, lightning-fast developments. Indeed, Siskiyou County would always be playing catch-up, struggling to reckon with the tsunami of the suddenly scaled-up, illicit cultivation on private property destined to shock so many of its residents silly.

Those intent on growing cannabis commercially for the underground market were determined to grab Vista's long-unsellable lots fast, before everyone and their uncle descended into Vista's bargain basement and jacked up the asking prices in the soon scorching red-hot seller's market. People, as if on steroids, snapped up the long-overlooked, affordable lots like a junk-food junkie grabbing potato chips.

Bidding wars

The lot-buying frenzy triggered bidding wars for Vista's more desirable, secluded lots. One neighbor, an early small-scale grower, was cashing out on land he'd bought five years earlier for $8,000. He hoped to get $85,000 for his super-remote lot off an otherwise uninhabited cul-de-sac. It had a tiny shack, water tank and an irrigation system on it. He didn't get the $85,000 he'd asked for; a bidding war broke out, and he ended up getting $105,000.

While it was hard to believe, unimproved lots, deemed useless in 2014 and going begging at $5,000, would be snapped up like prime real estate for $150,000 or more by 2021-2022, when buying fever reached its peak. (It declined just as quickly soon after, due to a series of adverse events, including the

2021 Lava Fire that devastated 10% of the parcels, and the ever-changing underground cannabis market price.)

Story of the Hmong

Although a handful of the new lot holders were white, the vast majority were Asian American, including Koreans, Laotians, Vietnamese, and later, Chinese and Taiwanese. Mainly, though, they were Hmong.

The Hmong (again, silent "H") are one of the larger minority ethnic groups in China (similar in population to the Uyghur and Manchu). Many fled south into neighboring Asian countries centuries ago, mainly to Laos and Viet Nam, after having endured long oppression and persecution by China's dominant Han rulers, not unlike the genocide of American Indians in the 1800s.

For several generations, many lived in the mountainous jungles of Laos, then a French colonial outpost. The French taxed them heavily, and the only viable cash crop they could grow in their region to meet the crushing tax demand was poppy flowers to supply the heroin market. There are horror stories of parents forced to give away a daughter into bondage to corrupt Laotian enforcers instead of paying the burdensome tax to avoid worse consequences. They grew poppies to survive, not as an inherently criminal enterprise. Heroin and morphine use were socially frowned upon.

Laws and their enforcement, at least as they affected them, were often historically so oppressive, first in China, then in Laos (what would America's be?), that it had no doubt been easy to develop a wary contempt for them. It had been ages since they'd had the opportunity to forge their own independent government with a fair-minded system of laws in place, so a disdainful regard for the law seemed to be ingrained in many. Convincing them that laws *could* be fair-minded and worthy of following, rather than inherently oppressive and corrupt, could be a futile effort. A case in point was the two Hmong, Chi Meng Yang and his sister, Gaosheng Laitinen. They were convicted for trying to bribe Siskiyou Sheriff Lopey with a million dollars to leave certain grows alone; they'd assumed he could be bought.

Early in the Vietnam War, the Hmong had been secretly recruited to help combat communist forces in Laos. Two of my Hmong neighbors, both about my age, showed me the vintage U.S. military ID cards they'd managed to save for 50 years; they bore images of young teens who looked too young to be fighting a war. One told me that, before he joined, skirmishes came so close he once witnessed one unfolding from his classroom window.

The U.S. Central Intelligence Agency looked the other way on their heroin trade, even helping smuggle the product to market (some say unknowingly). They needed the Hmong troops for the war effort in fighting the communists, and heroin was supporting their local economy.

Perhaps in the process, such overlooking in time created something of a Hmong acceptance, or at least reluctant tolerance, of any supposed illegal drug if there existed a lucrative market for it, and no decent-paying work could be found. No doubt like their forebears, they would have undoubtedly preferred growing bitter melon, mustard greens and squash than any controversial drug source, but circumstances and market realities didn't always support their druthers and the temptation of fast riches was strong.

Opium wars

Of course, it was the imperialistic British who, long ago in the mid-1800s, had pushed opium on the Chinese people as aggressively as any inner-city smack dealer. They wanted to trade with China for its teas and silks, but there was a trade imbalance, and the Chinese demanded payment in silver for the remainder. By creating a commodity demand once they got enough Chinese hooked on the opium (grown primarily in then-British India), they generated enough silver to buy the coveted items.

Maybe what was now emerging was only a kind of delayed consequence of white Europeans having pushed forbidden opium onto the Chinese people. Along with the drug-trade realities of the tragic Vietnam War, what was happening was possibly no more than the chickens coming home to roost.

Sitting ducks

The Hmong became sitting ducks the second after U.S. forces pulled out of Saigon on April 30, 1975; it left them at the mercy of the Viet Cong. Those known to have sided with Americans and allied forces were summarily killed. Two of my immediate neighbors told me they'd lost family members, shot as they ran for their lives. They hid in the mountainous jungles before making their way to refugee camps in Thailand, and eventually gained refugee status to come to the U.S., some 300,000 over time.

Though doubtless still reeling from the traumas endured, they must've held at least guarded hopes of making fresh new starts in the much-vaunted Land of the Free. They settled primarily in California, Minnesota, and Wisconsin. While some welcomed them with open arms, they were no doubt shocked by the rank racism and indifference of others.

Remarkably clannish, with a phenomenal one mind bordering on psychic (as perhaps any persecuted people might be, needing to work closely together for mutual survival), they longed to establish tight-knit communities like they'd known overseas. Though agriculture was in their bones, in the early years many lost out to Mexican migrants in Southern California's growing fields for lack of English-language skills and a sometimes slow adaptation to the radically different ways of the new homeland. While some over time matched their agricultural talents to the American market, and others entered mainstream jobs like factory work, services, and some climbed up to high-paying professional fields, others came to rely on welfare to get by. (Been there, done that.)

Mt. Shasta's vision factory at work

Now, the rural-friendly, farming-attuned people were getting swept up in Mt. Shasta's vision-a-minute factory and California's historic impending cannabis legalization. They wanted to believe they'd at last found a place where they could establish their own rural community. They poured life savings into it and hoped to support their new rough-and-ready community by cultivating and marketing unlicensed cannabis through underground channels. While some Hmong elders strongly frowned on such illicit pursuits, the momentum behind the cultivation of unsanctioned cash crops, again, proved too strong and tempting for many to resist.

It was, of course, a line of work that people of all colors and nationalities and financial classes were suddenly finding irresistible. A burgeoning national black market for cannabis was destined to leave the slowly emerging legal one in the shade. Their product could be sold far cheaper without the steep licensing fees, grow space requirements and multiple taxes to drive up its retail price.

In California, the eventual combined local, state excise, and state sales taxes could add as much as 40% to the cost of cannabis purchased at legal pot dispensaries, depending on the region. One might've thought that regulators would realize, duh, that this would guarantee that the black market would continue to thrive, perhaps like never before. But then, given that the differing bureaucracies and government agencies tend to act without a coordinated big-picture overview, this was perhaps hoping for the impossible.

Everybody loves pot

Countless adventurers would become part of the tidal wave of scaled illicit pot growing surging through California. All those pesky, numerous restrictions and regulations being devised, casual pot entrepreneurs boldly chose to ignore.

Siskiyou County, again, opted to ban commercial pot growing outside city limits, as was their right under the new state law: *One couldn't gain approval to grow commercial cannabis in the Vista even if willing to play by the rules, as the rules specifically prohibited it.*

Once legalized, ostensibly you could grow up to six plants on your own residential property for your own use, but that was it. Any more and one might invite trouble without a commercial license. Among other things, the new rules would, in most cases, reduce unlicensed commercial grows *of any size* from a criminal offense to a simple civil misdemeanor. At first, the relatively few hoop-house operators who got busted paid the $500 civil fine and were often busy replanting the next day. In recent years, though, harsh, seemingly selective law enforcement and excessive penalties were imposed on growers for having technically illicit structures and other infractions, along with the confiscation of the crop and the standard fine. This would prompt growers to get their lawyer in California State Court in 2025 to successfully end the over-punitive practice.

Pandemonium erupts

As spring 2015 progressed, the Vista was hopping with worlds more traffic than the place had *ever* seen. It was a genuine land rush, a feverish move onto Vista land, like something out of another era.

An example of the degree of frenzied pandemonium afoot: Driving along Placone Drive one day, I spotted some litter, pulled over on the left side, and stopped to pick it up, as was my wont. It had been a sleepy, narrow back road stretch for ages, probably often seeing fewer than a dozen cars a week traverse it. In the few seconds I stopped and stepped out, two vehicles came roaring out of nowhere. Their occupants, never slowing down, sped halfway off the road on the right to get by, like bats out of hell, leaving giant clouds of dust in their wake.

No doubt they were hightailing it to the realtor's office to stake their claims.

CHAPTER 26

Supplying a stoned and natural-healing nation

By 2010, California was already growing enough cannabis to supply over three-fourths of the national underground market. With increasingly lax medical marijuana laws allowing massive quantities to be legally grown, and only if selling it outside state-permitted channels becoming illegal, people grew pot like crazy. The value of legitimate in-state sales and illicit pot exports together soon eclipsed the state's combined production of almonds, dairy, walnuts, wine and pistachios.

While the warp-speed scramble to cultivate unlicensed, large-scale cannabis was no doubt an oft-told tale in possibly every one of California's 58 counties, Siskiyou was especially popular in 2015. It was a seriously rural, thinly populated county with a relatively low cost of living and cheap land. Some growers were getting chased out of neighboring Trinity and Shasta counties after authorities began crackdowns on illicit operations there. Many lots in Siskiyou's out-in-the-boonies subdivisions looked enticingly affordable.

Brief ground zero?

As it happened, long-obscure Mt. Shasta Vista was very possibly briefly ground zero in all of Northern California for the massive, new, illicit grows suddenly springing up on private property. The place offered some 1,200 remote, good-sized, undeveloped, dirt-cheap parcels for rapidly launching a group-coordinated cultivation enterprise such as the well-funded, unregulated entrepreneurs were systematically rolling out.

Sometimes becoming instant homesteaders as well, other times being daily or semi-daily commuters, the buyers snapped up the long-overlooked parcels in a frenzy, seeing them as steals (as, of course, had always been the case throughout the place's entire history). They sold like crazy to anyone willing to take a chance and bypass what would indeed prove to be the county's woeful unpreparedness and its all-but-unenforceable restrictive ordinances.

Ignoring the system

Even if the county *had* permitted commercial grows in the Vista, the flurry of new regulations meant that growers would've had to constantly deal with state and county agencies, tons of paperwork, regular inspections, strict bookkeeping, *individual tracking from seed to store*, fees, taxes, more fees, more taxes… *arghh!* Who needed that? But, as one new neighbor put it, rogue growers worked outside the cage; legal growers worked inside it. It was a cage either way.

If one could grow seas of green with little chance of getting busted, and, initially, a minor fine and rude crop seizure if so, to supply the thriving underground market already established in California and beyond, who wouldn't go for it? Besides people like me, that is. I valued tranquility and the peace of mind I felt for being law-abiding, knowing such dicey pursuits would destroy it in a heartbeat. Anyhow, I already had a thriving (and *legal*) cottage industry peddling local pumice stones nationwide online. (And a black thumb, besides; I managed to drown the one cannabis plant I bought on a lark at a Mt. Shasta dispensary.)

Although it has long since become a hackneyed comparison, illicit growing really was akin to brewing bathtub gin during Prohibition; the temptation to pursue quick riches proved irresistible to all sorts of otherwise perfectly law-abiding people.

Disturbing flashbacks

At first, the situation often made sporadic crop busts relatively little hassle, not much more than a speeding ticket. But not always. Periodic high-intensity raids by sheriff deputies and California National Guard units bearing assault rifles so terrified some growers, unaware that such hardball tactics could be employed in the U.S. to any so cavalier or naive as to ignore laws like they didn't exist, that it triggered PTSD in older Asian cultivators. They flashed back to the killing fields they'd barely managed to escape from with their lives. (Being a historically oppressed minority in an overwhelmingly white, quasi-good-ol'-boy local culture wouldn't help matters, either.)

The Vista's initial unlicensed commercial-scale cultivation efforts might be compared to having a fantastic run of luck playing the roulette wheel. Now and then, the winning streak was interrupted when the steel ball landed on 0 or 00, but growers managed to cover even those positions by setting up an informal crop insurance and legal-fees pool. Apart from the grief, loss of face and financial setbacks if busted, grow operations were assured of making a mint so long as the market held and one knew what they were doing. (Apparently, some would-be growers also lacked a green thumb.) The odds of winning on any given spin were 18 in 19, perhaps roughly the same as a cultivation not getting busted. Such fantastic odds proved too tempting for anyone willing to weather potential adversity to pursue the chance to make some serious fast money.

Anarchy-R-Us in the future state

A selective form of anarchy thus became acceptable for droves of people of all races, nationalities and socioeconomic backgrounds. It harked back to the earlier situation in the Vista (if on a far lesser scale), when people dropped anchor and ignored building codes like *they* didn't exist. Financially scrambling people wanting to get ahead were sorely tempted to take a chance and ignore laws and ordinances deemed unenforceable, arbitrary and unduly restrictive.

Obviously, Siskiyou County's old-guard citizens were more than a smidgen conservative. Their refusal to allow regulated commercial pot growing in the county's unincorporated area (along with 40 other counties, initially, about 69%) struck more open-minded residents as out of step with fast-changing times and growing awareness. Especially for happening in what was dubbed the future state, over time being the vanguard of a dizzying number of things, including: surfing, skateboarding, blue jeans, personal computers, AI, legalized *medical* cannabis, the counterculture movement, the entertainment industry, LGBTQ+ equality, eco-friendly clothing, stricter emission standards, sneakers, T-shirts as outerwear, topless dancing as non-wear, fast-food drive-thrus, motor inns…

…but not *recreational* cannabis.

It seemed almost as if the future state was mortified that four others and D.C. had beat it to the punch on something that should've been another slam-dunk first. So much so that, in their haste to reestablish their future-state standing, legislators got careless with the bill's details. It seemed odd that they didn't cobble together any more carefully considered, practical and effective policy, especially given the opportunity to observe how legalization was playing out elsewhere.

'You want it, you got it'

But, then again, it might've appeared state legislators were fearful of a meltdown of society and business as usual (plus concerns over increased health risks, as cannabis smoke was determined carcinogenic), if the long-dreaded weed became *too* easy and cheap to get and got *too* many stoned off their gourds too often. So they put up hurdles to any more unrestricted and affordable use through a flurry of steep seed-to-store regulations, sky-high dispensary start-up costs, and annual licensing fees administered by new, high-salaried bureaucratic overseers, all driving up the retail price of legal pot… and enabling the underground market to thrive better than ever.

The new laws no doubt struck some as unrealistic and maybe even naive, almost as if legislators had imagined the black market would magically evaporate once legalization took effect. As the new law of the land, obedient, law-abiding citizens everywhere would of course fall in line with the latest regulations for the *yerba buena*. (That's Spanish for 'good herb.' Considering that Yerba Buena was San Francisco's original name, and how in the Sixties denizens of the town's storied Haight-Ashbury scene came to venerate this one particular herb, the name would prove deliciously apropos.)

To growers unfamiliar with the finer and often convoluted points of law and perhaps holding more simplistic thinking, cannabis was either legal or it wasn't. If it were, in their black-or-white reasoning, there could be no restrictions on growing and selling it whatsoever.

'Welcome to Weed!'

The fact that the Vista was a half hour from Weed, California, wouldn't help matters any. Named after Abner Weed, early 20th-century lumber baron, the town's stony moniker was naturally long the butt of jokes and source of endless snickers. A town couple's popular mountain-photography and souvenir shop, the Weed Store, paid for their daughters' college educations by selling products that lightheartedly punned on the town's name. It came as no surprise, then, when that town's outlying regions became the early epicenter of unregulated seas of green, as hundreds of growers banded together to rapidly produce large-scale, unlicensed (and unlicenseable) cannabis.

'There's gold in California!'... again

The consequences would prove enormous for California when it decriminalized unsanctioned commercial growing. It reduced it to a civil misdemeanor, no matter *how* many plants one might grow, in most cases. It thus paved the way for the rallying cry "There's gold in California!" to be heard once again (green gold this time), 166 years after the historic 1849 rush. Word again spread like wildfire as would-be ambitious entrepreneurs were irresistibly drawn to the Golden State from across the nation and overseas. The state, once again a global billion-ton magnet, was attracting myriads from around the globe to the fabulous, new, once-in-a-lifetime opportunity. People who, with a bit of luck, hard work and a lot of derring-do, might become fabulously wealthy.

Still wound up after the Civil War; historic racism against Asian Americans in the U.S.

Asian attraction to California as a stepping stone to riches was, of course, nothing new. Beginning in 1849, Chinese immigrants, like other nationalities around the world, had flocked to the state they called Gum San, or "Gold Mountain", often to escape extreme poverty and political unrest at home. So many came, it led to widespread social disruption here — ostensibly over how Chinese were taking away jobs from whites for being willing to work more cheaply. But some historians maintain it was really about maintaining white purity.

Their presence and a growing belief in their unassimilability into Western culture fueled ugly racial violence. Feelings were still at fever pitch from the long Civil War, with all its racial tension. Incidents included major massacres of Chinese immigrants in Wyoming, Oregon and California — including one of the largest mass lynchings in U.S. history, in Los Angeles, in 1871. In 1882, U.S. President Chester Arthur signed the Chinese Exclusion Act, which would prohibit Chinese immigration to the United States for the next 61 years. It grew to restrict other Asian groups — including Japanese, Korean and Filipinos — by setting near-zero immigration quotas, before finally getting repealed in 1943. (Check out PBS's 2017 special by Ric Burns and Li-Shin Yu, *The Chinese Exclusion Act*.)

A recent example of continuing racial intolerance of Asian Americans in the U.S.: Sunisa Lee had just done her Hmong people proud by winning the 2020 Olympic Gold medal in women's gymnastics in Tokyo. She and her friends, all of Asian descent, were waiting for an Uber on an L.A. street a few months later when a carful of rowdies drove by shouting racial slurs and yelling, "Go back to where you came from!" One pepper-sprayed her arm.

Another, closer to home: Until ordered to stop by State Court as racial profiling, reportedly 19 out of 20 vehicles pulled over along the Vista's fronting 18-mile two-lane highway on one pretext or another held Asian American drivers. I was once pulled over, lights flashing, for making a U-turn at my highway mailbox, but was let off once the highway patrolman saw I was white. Had I not been, I suspect his eyes would've quickly scanned the inside of my vehicle to see if any drug-related items were in plain view and thus subject to seizure and probable-cause grounds for a warrantless search.

Shoulda gone fishing

Siskiyou County supervisors might just as well have gone fishing for all the dutiful compliance their eventual restrictive ordinances would muster, ordinances they no doubt liked to think of as newly chiseled in stone. The hundreds of new Vista lot holders had intuited that the ever-changing cannabis laws and ordinances to come would be untested and so prime candidates for being openly disregarded with little fear of consequence.

Especially if pursuing ambitious cultivation in the remote outbacks of Mt. Shasta Vista, with its chaotic and rebellious history and cheap parcels, making it an ideal place to go for the gusto. At first, individual parcel production exceeded the state's allowed six-plant personal-use limit by a factor of 12. Within a few years, as growers broke the once-tacit 99-plant limit agreement, production might exceed it by some 400-fold.

Asleep at the wheel

The massive land-buying and systematic cultivation efforts seemed to catch Siskiyou County officials flat-footed, asleep at the wheel, off guard, out to lunch, pick your metaphor. I briefly met the new code-enforcement officer, Jim Beam, at the Planning Dept. after the position was re-funded. He'd been pulled out of retirement from being a Yreka Fire Department officer. He struck me as one who indeed looked more ready to enjoy a day of fishing than tackle any wildly out-of-control, illicit pot-growing epidemic. His mindset was perhaps typical among officials' detached from what was going on, all hell breaking loose in the long-ignored Vista. "No one could've predicted such a thing would happen," opined one official to the media, head firmly in the sand.

Media alert

It was such an extraordinary development that the *Los Angeles Times* ran several feature stories on the unfolding phenomenon, and *The New York Times,* 3,000 miles away, did a piece on the town of Weed and its region's unlicensed pot-growing mania. For better or worse, the former, long-obscure, sleepy backwoods realm of Mt. Shasta Vista was having a moment — again. It had first caught the national eye two years earlier, in 2013. There had apparently already been enough pot growing and intrigue going on here to rate a segment in the Discovery Channel's sensationalist TV series, "Weed Country." (It undoubtedly gave would-be informal pot entrepreneurs ideas: "Hey, let's check out that place; it looks promising.")

But the Vista's long-festering plight — born of a county too provincial-minded and lackadaisical to keep up with fast-changing times, or (like most any place, probably) able to enforce its own ordinances and regulations should enough people opt to ignore them — had been careening on a collision course with reality for ages...

...until avoiding dealing with them at last proved to be an unwarranted luxury.

People had long predicted that Mt. Shasta Vista would be an unmitigated disaster. It came as no surprise then, when, a half century later, in largely self-fulfilling prophecy, they proved themselves absolutely right.

CHAPTER 27

Megachanges

Despite my being devastated, along with countless others, by the abrupt change in the once-sleepy backwoods, part of me found it at least encouraging to see the long-disregarded parcels finally appreciated and used; the half-century of development's stuck energy pattern was obliterated almost overnight. Fresh energies had given the place a new incarnation. But it felt as though the perennially wayward place had only traded one set of unsolvable problems for another.

I was stunned to see the single-minded pursuit of private gain through massive illicit grows turning the community, such as it was, upside down, at the expense of its established residents, the environment and civil order. The place had taken on a new, hyper-edgy energy. Although the odds were in favor of not getting busted, one never knew when their luck might run out. The result? Constant, wary vigilance.

It was heartbreaking to see the area's fragile ecosystem being so grievously disrupted and the land trashed… and the wildlife endangered. For decades, I'd often enjoyed hearing coyotes yipping up a storm in the distance, but had never seen one. I finally saw one, but it was dead. It had given up the ghost on my lot, bearing a frozen grimace of extreme agony. I felt certain it had ingested poison, probably from devouring a dead jackrabbit that had eaten toxins put out by one of the less thoughtful growers to prevent wildlife from sampling their product.

Stark raving mad

Like a few other longtime residents who weathered the megachanges rather than bail, I'd gradually adapt. But only after going stark raving mad. Being sound-sensitive, I'd moved here in part because the often-prevailing quiet was a balm for my nervous system, sensitive to begin with and shot to hell after long years on the hectic road. The frequent noise pollution from roaring generators, water pumps and barking dogs, and the sudden rush of traffic, especially the seemingly endless procession of noisy, fume-belching, barreling water trucks that I could hear coming a third mile off, pushed me over the edge. I tried to cancel out the decibel onslaught by cranking up ocean-wave sound devices, wearing a headset, and screaming at the top of my lungs until hoarse. Finally, as in The Doors' song, I'd break on through to the other side. But only after what felt like an eternity. Though profoundly saddened, I knew I'd adapt to the radically new situation.

I had considered moving, as most in fact did, but, in my sixties, the thought of uprooting after so long here and finding another place to live anywhere comparable was all but unimaginable for me. Besides, I'd settled here for life. Whereas many moved from town to town, or at least house to house, in growing up, sometimes state to state (even country to country), I grew up in the same city, the same house, *the same blinking room,* from birth until striking out on my own.

It had been a supreme struggle to adjust to any new environment while at the same time trying to earn a living. It had taken me seven years to shake free of the gravity field of my Presidio Heights Edwardian home in San Francisco and the Bay Area in general, another nine years before I finally felt at home in the Vista, despite living in structures I'd built with my own hands. It had taken sharing my place with rainbow family members a second time, in 1987, before I at last felt at home in my own house.

During the first months, the sudden flood of new neighbors kept behind their locked gates. This made it impossible to introduce myself and hopefully work through urgent concerns. Loud hellos at the gates went unheard or ignored. It would've been so much easier to adapt to the new situation if I'd actually met my new neighbors right away. But days, then interminable weeks, went by without any outreach. Hundreds of cars drove past my place as if I didn't exist; the Vista suddenly felt like a parallel universe in which some faceless invasion force had taken over.

A broken system; mutual forgiveness

Beside myself with anxiety, I, along with other concerned residents, filed flurries of formal written complaints with the Planning Department, where such complaints were then submitted as a civil matter, rather than with the Sheriff's Department. My writing hand went numb. But it was an exercise in futility. The new system couldn't *begin* to get a handle on the out-of-control situation. (I imagined the place's firstcomers in heaven watching the scene unfold and saying, "Now he knows how it feels.") Other counties issued self-abatement orders, which enabled one avoiding getting fined and one's illicit crops being forcibly and rudely chopped, no doubt enabling a far better compliance rate. But not our county.

Then, mercifully, things began to quiet down. People settled in. Generators whose drones were disturbing even to them were either swapped out with quieter models or muffled. Dogs quieted down as *they* settled in.

My more Western-assimilated neighbors (some spoke little or no English) finally introduced themselves. At that point, I withdrew all my complaints at Planning.

They were disarmingly friendly. But also a little guarded. After all, they didn't know if I was prejudiced, or if I'd accept what they were doing (perhaps not realizing I'd already filed complaints). They assured me they wanted to get along and would be sensitive to my needs and concerns. They asked only that I come to them with problems rather than call county authorities. Since I'd already bitten the bullet and had, perforce, changed my tune after realizing the authorities were essentially useless, I gladly agreed. If they could (albeit unknowingly) look past my having reported many before we met (or their predecessors, as lots often changed hands quickly), I could cut them serious slack for their bold enterprises. Obviously, I could no longer afford the luxury of standing on my principles in certain areas if we were to peacefully co-exist.

I always felt too chagrined to confess my futile attempt to try to keep them from growing here. I realized that, despite the extreme provocation in my mind justifying such desperate efforts, I'd become something of a fascist myself.

Some remained wary of me, seemingly beyond my having no skin in the game and not being a fellow Asian, as if sensing my zero-tolerance campaign of 10 years earlier. Karma's a bear.

Among the Hmong

The wife of one of my new neighbors, Ricky (Americanized name), several times brought over specially prepared vegetarian spring rolls, fresh from the oven; a neighbor had seldom been so thoughtful. My neighbor Chris gifted me with his extra jump box (which invention I didn't even know existed) after I asked for help with a dead battery. Another, Kee, stopped to share some delicious black cherries he'd scored. Yet others gave me generous amounts of bud from their first harvests. (I didn't know what to do with them, not having smoked the herb in decades, and it never having been my drug of choice; I was already naturally spacey, and had a bad reaction to all but the tiniest microdoses of THC.) I got invited to parties for a while, but didn't exactly fit in, for, beyond being the only white person, I was also a non-smoking, non-toking, non-drinking vegan, and not much of a party person to begin with.

While we don't often intermingle, living in different universes, as it were, I, a retiree no longer hustling to make a buck, unlike them, and they, a tight-knit group, both for being a historically persecuted minority in America and for openly flouting the law, for the most part we get along. Beyond the occasional roaring water truck, with only maybe half as many growing as in 2022, there's a quietude here once again. In some ways, it's even quieter than before, as my neighbors value tranquility and, unless riled, have a circumspect, quiet mindset, the same as me.

You became a philosopher

I gradually adjusted to the new intractable reality of the development and resigned myself to making the best of the situation that others had run away from screaming. (I'd elected to stay to do my screaming.) I resonated with the saying of Socrates about marriage: "If you get a good wife, you'll be happy. If you get a bad one, you'll become a philosopher." I'd long ago become a philosopher on joining the already discombobulated development that was now one more than ever.

Humankind is nothing if not adaptable.

Possibly in time, county pot ordinances will change. More likely, though, as the underground market becomes further saturated and the wholesale price declines, it might no longer pay to grow cannabis on such water-challenged land that requires every drop of the precious liquid to be trucked in at no small cost. Then, those still here who have come to love and respect the Vista and its potential to be a peaceful, law-abiding community might shift to more socially-accepted lines of work. (Or, again, the pot laws change.) The place could yet heal and become a no longer dysfunctional backwoods community, on a new, more grounded and integrated level. ("Yeah, right, and pigs will fly," I can hear people saying who are familiar with the long-beset realm.)

Burying the hatchet

Granted, it would take a big dose of mutual forgiveness and amazing grace, of burying the hatchet and outgrowing silly racial intolerance among its residents, the larger community and county officials alike to create such a positive turnaround. (But then, we are entering an age of miracles.) The years-long backlog of well-dwelling permits issued, for instance, could be remedied as the current no-way stance of county officials shifted to a more can-do one, clearing the way for people to become law-abiding residents and thus at last gain some long-desired peace of mind.

Pollyanna thinking? Wonky Vistan delusionality alive and well? Maybe.

The Big Sagebrush flourishing here, constantly purifying the land with medicine long recognized and used by Native Peoples, offers some hope. The sage (Latin name: *Artemisia tridentata)* has been scientifically proven to possess antimicrobial and antioxidant properties, which makes it ironic that a place where the healing plant flourished so prodigiously was ecologically devastated in recent times.

But by the same token, it gives hope that the land will more readily bounce back, mending itself, the way our self-healing planet does, rejuvenating over time, just like it did after Abner Weed was done harvesting the place's tall trees, with so many purifying plant factories at work. The land experienced by far the biggest baby-boom of new sage plants I'd ever witnessed in the spring of 2024: There were *thousands* of the tiny new plants sprouting up on my parcel alone. It was as if Earth was saying, "time to heal."

Synchronicity at work?

Was the Sixties' back-to-the-land euphoria reactivated by Vista's unheralded 50th anniversary?

To anyone giving credence to the existence of metaphysical realities and there being a grand synchronicity at work in the universe by an omniscient and loving Creator, I submit the following: The year 2015, being the golden jubilee of the Vista's founding, possibly served on the subtle to reactivate and further amplify the euphoric, topsy-turvy DNA of the place's founding an exact half century earlier. The excitement that was indelibly imprinted on the land by people first psyched over it being such a sweet spot to camp in, then retire at, then get back to the land at, was, 50 years later, possibly infused in a modern-day land rush of people who saw it as a great place to grow pot at, while at the same time developing a rough-and-ready Asian American community.

And that the time stream's exact moment — a confluence of the 50th anniversary with California's pending, long-anticipated pot legalization — possibly sparked the manifestation of yet another — one magnitudes more dizzying — incarnation of the Vista as an incurable dreamland. A community as blissfully unmindful and stubbornly disregarding of certain mundane realities as ever.

Something to ponder, in any event.

But whether one dismisses the convergence of events as mere coincidence or sees it as part of the grand synchronicity of an intelligent universe, no one will deny that the place experienced something quite extraordinary.

Or that the recent events, astonishingly outlandish as they seemed, were perhaps only Mt. Shasta Vista's latest chapter in its tattered book of misadventures writ large.

Afterword

The fifth century B.C. Chinese philosopher Lao Tse said that the cause of anything is everything, and the cause of everything is anything. Perhaps it could be thought simplistic to try to attribute what happened — or didn't happen — in Mt. Shasta Vista to specific causes. It's hard to say.

In any event, without verifying specific key facts, I'll never know with absolute certainty the *probable* trigger or triggers for the place's extraordinary unraveling over time. Namely, whether the land sold to developer Collins indeed created such an intense uproar among other family members and the community at large from the start that the place never had a chance. Or whether the power company in fact jacked the line-extension rates prohibitively soon after the first settlers moved in.

While I'm over 90% sure both are essentially true, I was of course left with a bit of doubt.

I called Pacific Power's Medford, Oregon office, hoping someone there would help clarify things. But after 20 minutes of wading through endless phone menus and futilely seeking a "speak to an operator" option, I knew I'd struck out: They didn't seem to want to talk to anyone (let alone someone who'd gotten by without their centralized go-juice for nearly half a century, thank you). I might've driven 350 miles to their headquarters in Portland and maybe stood a better chance of getting some definitive answer, but life is short.

And I might've tried contacting some members of the Martin family's current generations living in the area, to confirm or deny the circumstances of the sale. But I learned that some longtime residents have a reputation for being a bit cantankerous. I suppose a part of me was afraid that, if it were true, they'd still be so mad over how their uncle, or whoever it was, sold out his inheritance just so a bunch of outsider yahoos like me could live in their former treasured backwoods that they wouldn't even want to talk to me. That, or I'd be given a fresh, time-warped taste of the hell the firstcomers experienced. Another part of me hoped time had healed the hurt and they no longer held ill feelings towards the development, even such as it is now, but obviously the cynic won out.

Even so, hope springs eternal that one day there might again be peace in the valley.

About the Author

Stuart R. Ward, named after his father though the *last* of five sons, grew up in San Francisco during the 60s. Stir-crazy for living in the same room since birth until coming of age, he dharma-bummed around the nation for seven years, a human pinball in perpetual motion hitchhiking cross-country and riding the rails.

Wanderlust spent, he discovered Mt. Shasta Vista in 1978 and has been there ever since.

He dedicated 17 years to volunteering at the nearby Stewart Mineral Springs resort. He recently retired from a thriving cottage industry gathering pumice stones that wash down Mt. Shasta, wholesaling them nationwide online, primarily for skincare.

Previous self-published ventures include *Body Freedom Day: When a Clothed-Minded World Unraveled* and *Strange Days Indeed: Memories of the Old World*. This is his first purely nonfiction work.

Personal note

Thanks for reading. If you enjoyed this book and got it through an online bookseller, I'd love it if you could leave an honest 30-second review.

*"Books are never finished
— they are merely abandoned."*

—OSCAR WILDE

Praise for earlier works

Body Freedom Day:
When a Clothed-Minded World Unraveled

"… [A]n excellent counterpart in both form and subject to Edward Bellamy's Looking Backwards (1888)"

–LEE BAXENDALL,
FOUNDER OF THE NATURIST SOCIETY

Strange Days Indeed:
Memories of the Old World

"… [P]rovides a zany look at the way the world is, and then offers a vision of the way it could be."

–PHILLIP CARR-GOMM,
ENGLISH WRITER AND FORMER CHOSEN CHIEF OF
THE ORDER OF BARDS, OVATES AND DRUIDS